PAT BROWN, MBA

Financial Literacy For Divorcees

"From Separation to Stability-Your Financial Reset Plan"

ABRAM 47 BROWN

First published by AbramBrown47 2025

First edition

ISBN: 978-1-967737-16-1

This book was professionally typeset on Reedsy.
Find out more at reedsy.com

Contents

Why This Book Was Written

This book is personal.

My parents got divorced when I was young—before I even reached high school. But here's the thing: you wouldn't have known it. They didn't make a scene out of their separation. They didn't pit me and my brother against one another. They didn't miss birthdays, graduations, football games, or school meetings. If you saw them in the stands or at a parent-teacher conference, you'd assume they were still married.

And that's the part that's always stuck with me—not the divorce itself, but how they handled it. With maturity. With mutual respect. With consistency. They showed me that divorce didn't have to mean destruction. It could be a transition handled with grace.

Still, one thing I didn't see growing up—even in my own family—was *financial conversation* around divorce. The emotions were addressed. The parenting was handled beautifully. But the money? That part remained unspoken. Quiet. Off-limits. And that's true for so many people.

That's exactly why I wrote *Financial Literacy For Divorcees.*

Because even in the best-case scenarios—where two people separate peacefully and co-parent with excellence—money can still be confusing. It can still become a source of fear, shame, regret, or uncertainty. And for those whose divorces are messy, painful, or financially devastating? It can feel impossible to recover.

This book is here to change that.

It's not a legal guide. It's not a therapy workbook. It's a practical, real-world financial playbook for people who are navigating one of life's most personal and difficult transitions.

It's for the person who's starting over. The person who didn't handle the bills and suddenly needs to understand credit, cash flow, taxes, and insurance. The person who got blindsided financially and is trying to rebuild with dignity. The person who's been "holding it together" but knows they need help getting back on track.

This book is not about shame or blame. It's about strategy. It's about reclaiming confidence and clarity. It's about helping you build a life that's not just *surviving* the aftermath—but *thriving* on the other side.

My parents showed me that it's possible to walk through divorce without bitterness. This book is here to show you that it's possible to walk through the financial side without confusion.

If you're here, you're ready. Let's build from here—together.

How to Use This Book

First things first—take a breath. You don't need to know everything, and you don't need to fix everything overnight. This book isn't here to overwhelm you. It's here to walk with you, step by step, as you rebuild your financial foundation after divorce.

This is not a textbook.

It's not a lecture.

And it's not written in a way that assumes you already "should" know this stuff.

This is a guidebook—for real people navigating real-life transitions. It's written in plain language, with practical advice, relatable examples, and encouragement when you need it most. Think of it as a financial conversation with someone who gets it—someone who's been in the room, seen the paperwork, felt the stress, and knows how to move forward.

Here's how to get the most out of it:

You don't have to read it in order.

While the chapters do follow a logical flow, feel free to skip around. If you're overwhelmed by credit and need to tackle that first, jump to the credit chapter. If you're trying to budget before your next rent payment is due, head there first. This book is meant to meet you where you are—not force you into someone else's timeline.

Read with a pen or highlighter nearby.

Underline what hits home. Circle terms you want to look up again. Put stars next to the action steps you want to come back to. Make this book *yours*. Dog-ear pages. Write in the margins. Turn it into your personal financial blueprint.

Give yourself grace.

You are not "behind." You are not "bad with money." You're in a new chapter of life—maybe one you didn't expect—and you're doing something powerful by facing it head-on. Give yourself permission to learn. To grow. To mess up and try again.

Revisit chapters as your life evolves.

What you need right now may be different from what you need a year from now. That's okay. Come back to this book when you're ready to invest, buy a home, revisit insurance, or make a will. It's designed to be a tool you return to—not a one-time read.

Talk about what you're learning.

If you have friends going through divorce, or adult children who are watching you rebuild, share what you're picking up. Start conversations. Ask questions. The more we normalize financial literacy—especially in the wake of major life changes—the stronger our communities become.

Apply what makes sense for you.

Every situation is different. Not every tip or suggestion will apply to your exact circumstance. That's okay. Take what fits. Adapt it to your life. The goal is progress, not perfection.

Most importantly—use it with courage.

This book is here to help you make informed, empowered decisions. To help you stop second-guessing yourself. To give you the confidence to manage your money with clarity and control.

Because divorce may have changed your life—but it doesn't get to define your future.

You do.

So whether you read this book cover to cover in one weekend, or flip through it slowly over a year, know this: you're already doing something powerful. You're showing up. You're learning. And you're building something stronger—financially and personally—than what came before.

The Financial Literacy Gap After Divorce

Divorce isn't just emotional—it's financial. And for many, the moment the ink dries on the paperwork, a new and often unexpected reality sets in:

You're in charge now.

In charge of the bills.

In charge of the budget.

In charge of the savings, the taxes, the retirement accounts, the insurance policies, and all the financial decisions you may or may not have been part of during the marriage.

This shift can feel empowering—but let's be real—it can also feel terrifying.

Because here's the truth that most people don't talk about:

There's often a massive financial literacy gap after divorce.

Maybe you were the one who handled the money in the marriage—but now you're splitting assets, dealing with legal costs, and navigating a whole new tax bracket. Or maybe your ex handled most of the finances—and now you're looking at a mountain of unfamiliar terms, login screens, and monthly statements, wondering where to even begin.

You're not alone.

Too many smart, capable adults find themselves financially disoriented after divorce.

And it's not because they're irresponsible. It's not because they're bad with money. It's because most of us were never *taught* this stuff. Not in school. Not in our families. And certainly not in the heat of a separation.

In many marriages, roles are divided. One person takes on the bills, the investing, the budgeting, or the taxes—while the other carries different responsibilities. That division can work fine... until the relationship ends. Then suddenly, what was once "our money" becomes *your* money to manage—and maybe for the first time in years, or ever, you're flying solo.

This is the gap.

The financial literacy gap after divorce isn't just about numbers.

It's about confidence.

It's about knowing what to do with the information.

It's about rebuilding trust in yourself and your financial future.

You might be asking questions like:

- What do I do with the retirement account we split?
- Am I supposed to change the beneficiaries on my life insurance?
- Can I still afford the house—or should I sell it?
- How do I build credit in my name again?
- What happens to the debt we shared?
- How do I create a budget when everything's changed?

These are the questions that swirl in your head late at night while you're trying to sleep—or in the quiet moments between signing documents, managing your household, or picking up the pieces.

And this is where financial literacy becomes your lifeline—not just to survive, but to *stabilize, recover,* and *thrive.*

This book was written to bridge that gap.

Not with fancy jargon. Not with judgment. But with **real talk, plain language, and practical steps** you can take to feel in control again.

Because whether you initiated the divorce, didn't see it coming, or mutually agreed to part ways, **your financial future is now yours to shape**.

That's not a threat—it's an opportunity.

You can build savings.

You can rebuild credit.

You can buy property, invest wisely, plan for retirement, protect your income, and create the kind of financial clarity that gives you peace of mind.

No matter what happened in the marriage or how messy the divorce got—this is your chance to reclaim the money part of your story.

The financial literacy gap is real.

But you don't have to live in it.

You can cross it, one step at a time.

And this book? It's your bridge.

The Goal: From Surviving to Thriving

Let's be honest: divorce can feel like being dropped in the middle of a storm with no umbrella and no map. For a while, you're just trying to stay upright. You're patching holes, managing emotions, keeping the lights on, and doing your best to show up for yourself, your kids, your job—even when your world feels upside down.

That's survival.

And sometimes, survival is a victory.

But let's be clear—that's not where your story ends.

Because survival might be the starting point, but **thriving** is the goal.

Thriving means you're no longer just reacting—you're planning.

You're no longer afraid of looking at your bank account—you're checking it with confidence.

You're not just "getting by"—you're building something. A new life. A new rhythm. A new sense of what's possible.

After divorce, a lot of people think the best they can do is damage control. That they'll always be catching up. That they'll never feel financially safe again. And that belief can stick around for years if no one interrupts it.

This book is here to interrupt it.

Because you are not doomed to live in reaction mode forever.

You can rebuild your savings.

You can rebuild your credit.

You can own property in your name.

You can invest for your future.

You can teach your kids what financial empowerment looks like.

You can look back one day and say, *"That chapter didn't break me. It built me."*

Thriving looks different for everyone.

For some, it's having a fully funded emergency account for the first time.

For others, it's buying a home in your name.

Maybe it's setting boundaries with financial requests from others.

Maybe it's finally understanding your investments—or feeling proud when you file your taxes on your own.

Thriving isn't about having it all together. It's about **gaining control**, **growing confidence**, and **making moves on your own terms**.

This book is your guide to that journey. It's here to give you the tools, language, and steps that weren't taught before—and probably weren't offered during your divorce.

It's here to remind you that your financial identity didn't disappear with your relationship. In fact, now is when it really gets to shine.

You're not starting over with nothing.

You're starting over with experience.

So yes, we're going to talk about budgets and insurance and investments and wills and taxes and credit cards. But we're also going to talk about something bigger:

Your peace of mind. Your agency. Your future.

Because you deserve more than just a survival plan.

You deserve a blueprint for the life you want to build—and the legacy you want to leave behind.

Part 1: Before the Papers – Financial Prep for Separation

Before the signatures. Before the court dates. Before the hard conversations about who gets what—there's a crucial phase that too many people skip: **financial preparation**.

Part 1 of this book is your early warning system. It's here to help you **get organized, protect yourself, and start thinking with clarity** before emotions, stress, or legal processes take over.

Whether you're the one initiating the separation or you sense the relationship is heading in that direction, this section walks you through the foundational steps that can make all the difference later. Because when it comes to divorce, **what you do before the paperwork is filed can shape your financial future for years to come**.

In this section, you'll learn how to:

- **Take inventory of your assets and debts** (what you own and what you owe)
- **Gather key financial documents** like tax returns, pay stubs, bank statements, and insurance policies
- **Open accounts in your name** and start establishing independent financial identity
- **Understand joint accounts and liabilities**, and what to do before things get messy
- **Create a personal budget** for the "now" and the "what's next"

- **Start building a support team**—including legal, financial, and emotional professionals
- **Set boundaries** around spending, communication, and shared resources during the transition
- **Think ahead** to custody, housing, health care, and insurance changes that will impact your financial world

This part of the book is not about fear—it's about **readiness**.

Because the more you know going in, the stronger you'll be coming out.

This is your financial head start.

This is where you stop reacting and start reclaiming your power.

And most of all, this is where your new chapter quietly, intentionally begins—**with knowledge, dignity, and a plan.**

Chapter 1: The Money Conversation – Facing What's Ahead

Let's start with this: if you're reading this chapter, you're probably dealing with one of the most emotional and disorienting transitions of your life. Whether your divorce is fresh, in progress, or finalized, money is probably sitting at the center of your stress. You're not alone.

Divorce brings a flood of emotions—grief, confusion, anger, maybe even relief. But while your heart is healing, the bills don't stop. The rent still comes due. Groceries still need to be bought. And decisions still need to be made.

This chapter is where we gently start to face what's ahead. No shame. No judgment. Just clarity, strategy, and compassion. We're not rushing anything here. We're just taking that first brave breath and saying, "Okay, let's figure this out."

Why the Money Conversation Is So Hard

Money has never just been about math. It's about history, habits, and emotion. And in marriage, finances can be deeply entangled—not just in bank accounts, but in roles, expectations, and sometimes unspoken power dynamics.

Maybe your ex handled the bills while you focused on the kids. Maybe you made more, and now you're worried about alimony or child support. Maybe you both earned money, but you never talked openly about where it went.

Whatever your financial story was during the marriage, now is the time to step into a new role: financial CEO of your life.

And that starts with a conversation. Not with your ex—at least not yet. But with yourself.

Step One: Take Inventory Without Judgment

Before you can make any smart moves, you need to know where you stand. That means facing the numbers—all of them.

Make a list:

- Your income (job, side gigs, benefits, etc.)
- Your expenses (fixed and variable)
- Your debts (credit cards, loans, joint accounts)
- Your assets (cash, property, retirement accounts)

Don't worry about what the numbers "should" be. Just get the facts down. Think of it like stepping on the scale before starting a new health plan. This is your financial starting point—not your finish line.

Tip: Use a notebook, spreadsheet, or budgeting app. Do what feels natural. The point is to see the full picture in one place.

Common Reactions (And How to Work Through Them)

Facing your finances after divorce can bring up:

- Shame: "How did I let it get like this?"
- Guilt: "I should have been more involved."
- Fear: "What if I can't make it on my own?"

Let me pause you right here: those thoughts are normal. But they are not facts.

You are not your mistakes. You are not doomed. You are not broken.

You are becoming. Becoming wiser. More aware. More resilient. More capable.

Start Building Your Financial Support Team

Even if you're doing this alone, you don't have to be alone. Start thinking about your team:

- A **family law attorney** if you're still in the legal process
- A **financial advisor** who can help you look long-term
- A **therapist** who can help you unpack the emotional weight of money
- A **trusted friend or mentor** to talk things through

You are now the CEO. Every CEO has advisors. This is your boardroom.

Embrace the Power of Small Wins

Right now, it might feel like there's a mountain ahead. But you don't climb a mountain in one leap. You climb it one step at a time.

Some small wins you can aim for this week:

- Open a checking account in your name (if you haven't already)
- Pull your credit report (free at annualcreditreport.com)
- Make a list of your monthly expenses
- Cancel one unnecessary subscription
- Talk to someone you trust about your financial situation

Celebrate these steps. They matter. They build momentum.

What If You're Behind?

Maybe you're in debt. Maybe you don't have savings. Maybe you've never invested a dime.

That's okay.

This book isn't about where you should have been. It's about where you can go next. And I promise: it is never too late to get your financial house in order.

Pros and Cons of Financial Independence After Divorce

Pros:

- Full control over your financial decisions
- Freedom to set your own goals and priorities
- Opportunity to learn and grow

- Rebuilding confidence and legacy

Cons:

- The learning curve can feel steep
- Managing everything solo can be overwhelming
- Emotional triggers tied to money may surface

But remember: the pros become stronger the more time you invest in learning.

Action Steps: Your First Financial To-Do List

1. List all income sources
2. Track every monthly expense
3. Pull your latest credit report
4. Identify and document all debts
5. Open a solo bank account
6. Choose a safe space to keep your financial documents
7. Set a 30-minute weekly money check-in with yourself

Don't try to do it all in one day. But do commit to starting.

Final Thoughts: This Is the Beginning of Something Stronger

You are not behind. You are not too late. You are not broken.

This is not just a financial chapter. It's a healing one.

You are learning how to stand in your own power. And that starts with one honest conversation: "Where am I, and where do I want to go?"

The next chapters will walk you through everything from credit and budgeting to investing and protecting your future. But this chapter is the foundation. The moment you chose to face it.

You're already doing it. One step, one page, one truth at a time.

Welcome to your new beginning. You've got this.

Chapter 2: What's Ours, What's Mine – Understanding Marital Property

When the dust starts to settle after a separation or divorce, one of the first questions that comes up is: what's mine, what's theirs, and what's ours?

It's a question that's both emotional and financial. Because it's not just about the things you bought together—it's about the life you built, the memories attached to those things, and the future you're now trying to protect. It's heavy. And that's okay. This chapter is here to help you understand the rules of the game so you can begin dividing what needs to be divided with a clear head, a strong heart, and a plan.

What Is Marital Property?

Let's start with the basics. Marital property is everything that you and your spouse acquired during your marriage. That means income, property, debt, investments—all of it. If it came into your life while you were legally married, odds are it's marital property.

It doesn't matter who earned it. If you were married when the paycheck hit the account, it's usually considered shared. If one person's name is on the car, but it was bought during the marriage? Still shared. This is one of those times where what "feels" fair and what the law says can be two different things.

Separate Property vs. Marital Property

Separate property is usually:

- Anything you owned before you got married
- Inheritances or gifts given specifically to you (not both of you)
- Certain personal injury settlements
- Anything that you and your spouse agreed in writing would remain separate (like in a prenup)

BUT (and it's a big but): if you mix your separate property with marital property, it can lose its separate status. This is called "commingling."

Example: You inherited $20,000 from your aunt and put it into a joint account. Then you and your spouse used that money for a down payment on your home. That money might now be considered marital property.

Action Step: Take Inventory

Before you start drawing lines down the middle, take inventory of everything you and your spouse own. Get it all on paper. This includes:

- Bank accounts
- Investment accounts
- Retirement accounts
- Real estate
- Vehicles
- Business interests
- Valuable personal property (jewelry, art, collectibles)
- Debts (credit cards, student loans, mortgages, personal loans)

Use a spreadsheet or a notebook. Just get it written down. This will help you and your attorney figure out what's marital, what's separate, and what might need to be negotiated.

How State Laws Impact Property Division

There are two major systems in the U.S. for dividing property in a divorce:

Community Property States: (like California, Texas, Arizona) Everything acquired during the marriage is split 50/50. Period.

Equitable Distribution States: (the rest of the country) The court divides things "fairly," which doesn't always mean equally. A judge considers factors like who earned what, who managed the home, the length of the marriage, and each spouse's financial situation.

Pros and Cons of Going Through Court vs. Mediation

Court: Pros:

- Enforces decisions when emotions run high
- Provides structure when communication has broken down

Cons:

- Expensive and time-consuming
- Public record
- The judge has final say (not you)

Mediation: Pros:

- More privacy
- More control over the outcome
- Often less expensive

Cons:

- Requires cooperation and willingness to compromise
- Not legally binding until finalized in court

What About the House?

The family home is often the most emotionally charged asset. There are usually three options:

- One person buys out the other
- You sell the home and split the proceeds
- You keep the home jointly for a time (not common, but possible)

Ask yourself: Can I really afford this home on my own? Or am I trying to hold on to something that's keeping me financially stuck?

What Happens to Retirement Accounts?

Yes, even your retirement account can be considered marital property. IRAs, 401(k)s, pensions—all of it. If you or your spouse contributed to it during the marriage, that portion may need to be divided.

This is often done using a document called a QDRO (Qualified Domestic Relations Order). It allows a retirement account to be split without penalties or tax consequences.

Action Step: Ask your attorney or financial advisor about QDROs and start the paperwork early. These take time to process and are often delayed.

Debt Counts Too

Just like assets, debt gets divided too. If the debt was incurred during the marriage, it may be shared—even if only one person signed for it.

This includes:

- Credit cards
- Personal loans
- Auto loans
- Medical debt
- Student loans (this one varies state to state)

Action Step: Run a credit report. This helps you catch any debts you may have forgotten or didn't know about.

Tips for Protecting What's Yours

- Don't move or sell anything major before discussing it with your attorney
- Don't try to hide assets. Courts don't play games, and it can hurt your case
- Keep copies of all financial documents
- Open your own bank account and start separating finances gradually

Emotional Attachments vs. Financial Wisdom

You may feel emotionally attached to the house, the car, or even the wedding china. But emotions can cloud good financial judgment. Just because you love something doesn't mean it's worth fighting over.

Ask yourself:

- Does this item hold long-term value?
- Will it bring me peace or stress?
- Can I afford the upkeep?

Sometimes the smartest move is letting go.

Final Thoughts: Reclaiming What Matters

Understanding marital property is one of the most important steps in reclaiming your financial independence. It's not just about dividing things up—it's about deciding what you want to carry forward into your next chapter.

You don't have to rush this. Take it one decision at a time. Gather your information. Lean on trusted professionals. And know that you are more than the things you shared or the debts you once carried.

You are building a new financial life—one step, one asset, one decision at a time.

And you're doing better than you think.

Chapter 3: Gathering Documents – What You'll Need to Prepare Financially

Let's take a breath. You're here. That's a win.

Maybe the papers aren't signed yet. Maybe you're in the thick of it. Maybe you're sitting on the other side, trying to make sense of what comes next. No matter where you are in this process, gathering the right financial documents is one of the most important things you can do to reclaim your power.

This chapter is your personal checklist, your roadmap, your calm in the storm. Because the truth is, paperwork can feel overwhelming when you're already emotionally maxed out. But every form, every statement, every number is a step toward clarity—toward protecting your interests and securing your future.

Why Gathering Documents Early Matters

You can't divide what you don't understand. You can't plan for the future if you don't know where you stand today. And you absolutely can't advocate for yourself if you're walking into a negotiation blind.

When you gather your documents early, you:

- Create a clear snapshot of your finances
- Prevent delays in legal and financial proceedings
- Spot missing or hidden assets

- Begin to take emotional ownership of your financial life

It might feel like you're just doing paperwork, but really, you're planting the seeds for your financial independence.

Core Categories of Documents You Need

Let's break it down. You want to gather documents in the following areas:

Income

- Pay stubs (last 3–6 months)
- W-2 forms from the last 2 years
- 1099 forms for freelance or contract work
- Tax returns (last 2–3 years)
- Business income (P&L statements if self-employed)

Assets

- Bank statements (checking, savings)
- Retirement accounts (401k, IRA, pensions)
- Investment accounts (brokerage, mutual funds)
- Property deeds or titles (home, car, land)
- Life insurance policies with cash value
- Valuable personal property (art, jewelry, collectibles)

Liabilities (Debt)

- Mortgage statements
- Car loans
- Credit card balances and statements
- Personal loans
- Student loans
- Lines of credit

Household Expenses

- Utility bills
- Grocery bills or budgeting software printouts
- Childcare expenses
- Medical bills and insurance premiums
- Subscriptions and memberships

Legal Documents

- Prenuptial or postnuptial agreements
- Trust documents
- Wills and estate plans
- Divorce filings or legal correspondence

How to Gather If You Don't Have Access

Sometimes, especially in contentious or controlling relationships, one partner has limited access to the financial information. If this is your situation, take these steps:

- **Start with what you can access**: Log into accounts that are in your name or that you can legally access.
- **Request copies**: Ask your attorney or the court to subpoena documents if your spouse refuses to share.
- **Pull your credit report**: This can help you spot debts you didn't know about.
- **Document everything**: Take screenshots, save PDFs, or print documents and keep them in a safe, private place.

Organizing Your Documents

Having the documents is step one. Keeping them organized is step two.

- **Use folders or binders**: Create physical or digital folders by category.
- **Label clearly**: Include the account name, date, and what it is.
- **Back up everything**: Use cloud storage or an encrypted flash drive.
- **Update regularly**: Things will change month to month. Keep your files current.

Pros and Cons of Professional Help

Hiring a Certified Divorce Financial Analyst (CDFA), accountant, or financial planner can be a huge help during this stage.

Pros:

- Helps you spot red flags
- Can do the heavy lifting
- Explains what each document means
- Gives you peace of mind

Cons:

- Can be expensive
- Not always necessary if you're financially savvy
- Finding a good one takes time

Action Steps

- Create a master list of needed documents
- Schedule an hour each day (or week) to collect them
- Save everything in one secure place
- Highlight any missing items and request them

- Share copies with your attorney or financial professional

Emotional Roadblocks and How to Overcome Them

- **Procrastination**: Set a timer and start with 15 minutes.
- **Overwhelm**: Break it into categories and tackle one at a time.
- **Fear of discovering something painful**: Remember, truth gives you power.

You are not alone in feeling nervous, confused, or even ashamed about your financial documents. But collecting them is not about being perfect. It's about being prepared.

Final Thoughts

This process isn't about revenge. It's about clarity. It's about knowing what you have, what you owe, and what your options are. It's about stepping into the next phase of your life informed, confident, and in control.

Keep going. You're doing the hard work that your future self will thank you for. You're not just collecting documents.

You're collecting power.

Chapter 4: Protecting Yourself Before You File

Before the paperwork is even signed, before the word "divorce" leaves your lips in a courtroom, there is a moment of pause—a moment where everything feels uncertain. Maybe you're thinking about separating. Maybe you've already decided that divorce is the next step. But before any legal forms are filed, before you even hire an attorney, there's something even more important that needs to happen: you need to financially protect yourself.

Let's be real: this chapter isn't about fear—it's about preparation. It's about arming yourself with the knowledge and tools that allow you to walk into the next chapter of your life with clarity, control, and calm. You don't need to be rich. You don't need to be a financial genius. You just need to be informed.

Why This Step Is Crucial

Protecting yourself before filing isn't about being sneaky. It's about being smart. It's about recognizing that once the divorce process officially begins, the rules change. Courts may freeze certain accounts. Emotions run high. People do things out of spite. What you do now—quietly and calmly—can determine whether you're playing defense the whole way through, or whether you're positioned with strength from the jump.

Take Inventory of Your Finances

Before anything else, you need a clear view of what exists. That includes:

- Checking and savings accounts
- Investment accounts
- Retirement accounts
- Credit cards and personal lines of credit
- Mortgages, car loans, and other debts
- Insurance policies (life, auto, home, health)
- Real estate or property
- Any valuable items (jewelry, artwork, collectibles)
- Business interests

Make copies of all account statements for the past 12 months. Print them out or save them digitally with backup. You're not hiding anything—you're preserving a record. This becomes critical later if anything "goes missing" or someone conveniently forgets how much was in the joint account.

Check Your Credit Report

Go to AnnualCreditReport.com and pull reports from all three bureaus (Equifax, Experian, and TransUnion). You're looking for:

- Debts in your name
- Joint accounts you forgot about
- New credit lines you didn't authorize
- Accounts your spouse may have opened using your name

This is your financial fingerprint. Know what's there so no one can use it against you later.

Open Accounts in Your Name Only

If you don't already have them, open a:

- Checking account
- Savings account
- Credit card

Use a bank your spouse doesn't use, and have statements sent to a secure location (email, PO Box, or trusted friend/family). This is about building your individual identity again. Even if you don't fund these accounts right away, you're laying the groundwork for separation.

Establish a Budget for Separation

You may still be in the same household, but mentally, you're preparing for two separate financial lives. Start a mock budget based on your income and what you expect your living expenses to be post-separation. Include:

- Rent or mortgage (for your new space if applicable)
- Utilities
- Food
- Insurance
- Childcare or school expenses
- Transportation
- Minimum debt payments

This helps you identify what kind of support or division of assets you'll need to negotiate.

Secure Access to Important Documents

Gather and safely store:

- Birth certificates (yours and your children's)
- Marriage certificate
- Social Security cards
- Tax returns (at least 3 years)
- Property deeds or lease agreements
- Vehicle titles
- Health insurance cards and policies
- Estate planning documents (wills, trusts, powers of attorney)

Scan them. Back them up. If you need to, keep them at a trusted friend's house or safe deposit box. Don't assume you'll have access to these later.

Change Passwords and Set Up Digital Security

Update passwords for:

- Email
- Bank accounts
- Cloud storage (Google Drive, iCloud)
- Social media
- Any shared apps with stored payment info (Amazon, Netflix, etc.)

Use two-factor authentication wherever possible. This is about protecting your digital life. You don't want a soon-to-be-ex snooping in your financial plans, messages, or emails with your attorney.

Understand Joint Liability

One of the biggest traps in divorce is joint debt. If both names are on a credit card or loan, the creditor doesn't care who used it—they can come after you both. Even if a divorce decree says your ex is responsible, the lender can still go after you if your name is on it.

Action Step: Work to separate joint accounts before you file. Pay them off, transfer balances, or at minimum, freeze additional charges.

Prepare Emotionally for Financial Pushback

If money was a power dynamic in your marriage, things may get tense. If your spouse made more, controlled the accounts, or discouraged your financial independence, be prepared for some resistance. That doesn't mean back down. It means know your rights and build a team (attorney, financial advisor, therapist) who can support you through it.

Don't Rush to File If You're Not Ready

It might feel empowering to just file and be done with it—but if you're not financially prepared, that move can backfire. Take the time to:

- Build a cash cushion
- Gather your documents
- Plan your exit

This isn't stalling—it's strategizing.

Avoid Financial Retaliation

Unfortunately, some spouses will:

- Drain bank accounts
- Max out credit cards
- Stop paying bills
- Cancel insurance

You can't always prevent this, but you can reduce your risk by separating accounts, monitoring your credit, and speaking with an attorney about temporary court orders that protect you financially.

Pros and Cons of Pre-Filing Protection

Pros:

- Gives you a head start on rebuilding
- Reduces the chance of financial sabotage
- Puts you in a position of strength

Cons:

- May create tension at home
- Can feel overwhelming without help
- Requires time and planning

But the pros far outweigh the cons when it comes to protecting your long-term future.

Final Encouragement

You may feel like you're preparing for war—and in some ways, divorce can feel that way. But this isn't about battle. It's about building your safety net. It's about protecting your energy, your time, and your financial life so that when the next chapter begins, you're not starting from scratch—you're starting from solid ground.

You've got this. And you don't have to do it alone.

What you do now matters more than you know. Take the steps. Make the calls. Get your documents. Create your plan. One step at a time.

Because this isn't just the end of something. It's the beginning of something stronger, wiser, and entirely yours.

Chapter 5: The Divorce Team – Choosing the Right Lawyer, Mediator, and Advisor

When you're going through a divorce, it can feel like you're stuck in the middle of a high-stakes chess match with no clear strategy, no coach, and no idea what your next move should be. Everything is personal, but at the same time, it's all business. It's emotional, but it's also deeply financial. This is why building the right team around you matters—not just to survive this season, but to come out of it with a clearer path forward.

This chapter is about choosing the right professionals to support you—your divorce team. Your lawyer. Your mediator. Your financial advisor. Maybe even your therapist. Because let's be real: no one should walk through this process alone.

The Emotional Weight of Decision-Making

Let's start by acknowledging something: making clear, rational decisions in the middle of emotional upheaval is hard. Your heart is heavy. You might be angry, sad, or just plain exhausted. That's why your team matters so much. The people you surround yourself with during a divorce can either help you stay grounded and forward-focused—or they can stir the pot, rack up your costs, and leave you more confused than when you started.

Your job right now is to build a team that helps you stay calm, informed, and empowered.

The Attorney: Legal Muscle Meets Strategic Mindset

Choosing a divorce attorney isn't just about hiring a fighter. It's about hiring a strategist. Someone who knows the law, yes—but also someone who knows how to communicate, compromise, and keep you out of court when it's avoidable.

Ask yourself:

- Do I want a bulldog or a problem-solver?
- Am I looking to win every point, or walk away with dignity and financial stability?

Pros of Hiring an Experienced Divorce Lawyer:

- They understand the ins and outs of divorce law in your state
- They can advocate for you in court if needed
- They know how to negotiate on your behalf

Cons:

- High hourly rates can quickly add up
- Some lawyers may escalate conflict unnecessarily
- You may feel like you're handing over control of your case

How to Choose:

- Interview at least 2–3 attorneys before deciding
- Look for someone who listens more than they talk
- Ask how they handle high-conflict situations
- Check online reviews and ask about their past cases

Action Step: Make a list of qualities you want in an attorney. Then set up consultations and come prepared with questions—about their experience, their philosophy, and how they bill.

The Mediator: Bridging the Divide

A mediator is a neutral third party who helps you and your ex work through the terms of your divorce outside the courtroom. Mediation can save time, money, and a lot of emotional stress.

It's especially helpful when:

- You both want to avoid court
- You believe compromise is possible
- You have kids and want to keep the peace

Pros:

- Cost-effective compared to litigation
- Typically faster than going through court
- Encourages cooperation and healthy communication

Cons:

- Doesn't work well in highly combative situations
- Mediators don't offer legal advice
- Not legally binding until you draft a final agreement

How to Choose:

- Look for someone certified in family mediation
- Ask about their experience with cases like yours
- Find someone with a calm demeanor and excellent communication skills

Action Step: If you and your ex are on relatively civil terms, explore mediation early. It can lead to less bitterness and more control over the outcome.

The Financial Advisor: Making the Money Make Sense

A financial advisor who understands divorce isn't just about stocks and bonds. They're about strategy. Tax planning. Asset division. Retirement accounts. Insurance.

This is especially critical if:

- You weren't the one managing the money during the marriage
- You have retirement accounts to split
- You're not sure what a "fair" division really looks like

Pros:

- They help clarify the financial picture
- They can show you the long-term impact of your decisions
- They help you rebuild post-divorce with smart planning

Cons:

- You may need to pay for their time or ongoing services
- Not all advisors are well-versed in divorce matters

How to Choose:

- Look for a Certified Divorce Financial Analyst (CDFA) or a CFP with divorce experience
- Ask how they've helped clients navigate divorce
- Make sure they're fiduciaries (legally bound to act in your best interest)

Action Step: Start with a financial inventory. Know what you have, what you owe, and what your lifestyle costs. Bring this info to your advisor so they can help you build a game plan.

Bonus Team Members to Consider

Therapist or Divorce Coach: Someone who can help you process emotions and make rational decisions.

Estate Planning Attorney: You may need to update your will, beneficiaries, power of attorney, etc.

Accountant: Especially if your taxes are complicated or if you'll be filing separately for the first time in years.

A Word About Friends and Family

Your inner circle may be full of opinions. Some will mean well. Some will be messy. Some will want to "take your side" and feed your anger.

Here's the thing: during divorce, emotions are already running high. Choose the voices you let in carefully. Trust people who:

- Stay calm
- Encourage peace
- Want what's best for you, not what's worst for your ex

Final Thoughts: You Deserve a Team That Respects You

Divorce isn't a solo sport. And it doesn't mean you're weak for needing support. In fact, assembling the right team might be the strongest move you can make.

Your lawyer helps protect your rights. Your mediator helps preserve your peace. Your financial advisor helps protect your future.

Build your divorce team like you would build a starting lineup—with intention, balance, and trust. The right team doesn't just help you get through this process. They help you rise after it.

And you will rise. You'll rebuild. You'll redefine. And you'll realize, maybe for the first time in a long time, just how strong you really are.

Chapter 6: Avoiding Emotional Financial Mistakes

Divorce is a whirlwind. It doesn't just flip your life upside down emotionally—it can knock your financial stability out from under you too. And here's the truth most people don't talk about: when emotions run high, financial decisions often run low. That's not a knock on your intelligence. It's just human nature. When your world feels uncertain, it's easy to make choices from a place of hurt, anger, fear, or guilt instead of from a place of wisdom, clarity, or strategy.

This chapter is about helping you slow down, breathe, and make better money decisions even in the middle of emotional chaos. Because your future depends on it. And you deserve a future that feels grounded, not reactionary.

The Emotional Minefield of Divorce

Let's name it: Divorce is grief. It's fear. It's heartbreak. It's sometimes rage. All of that is real, and all of it deserves space. But what those emotions don't deserve is your retirement savings, your credit score, your house, or your long-term peace.

Financial decisions made in moments of emotional intensity often come with long-term consequences. That's why awareness is your first line of defense. If you can name what you're feeling and give yourself a pause before making a financial move, you've already won half the battle.

Common Emotional Money Mistakes to Watch For

Spite Spending: You want to prove something to your ex. So you take a lavish trip, buy the luxury car, or max out a credit card on a "revenge wardrobe."

Emotional Giving: You feel bad for your kids or want to make up for the instability. So you overcompensate with gifts, tech, or new experiences you can't afford.

Avoidance: You don't open your mail. You ignore bills. You tell yourself, "I'll deal with it later."

Impulse Selling: You sell off investments or property just to cut ties, not realizing you're taking a major financial hit.

Withholding Information: You try to control the narrative by hiding assets or not disclosing full financial details. This can backfire in court and damage credibility.

Emotional Attachment to Assets: You want to keep the house because it holds memories, even though maintaining it will put you underwater financially.

How to Make Smarter, Calmer Financial Decisions

1. **Don't Rush Big Moves** Unless it's urgent (like paying your mortgage), press pause. Give yourself a cooling-off period before any major decision. Create a 48-hour rule for purchases, sales, or financial commitments.
2. **Get a Financial Ally** Find someone you trust who can walk through decisions with you. This could be a financial advisor, a divorce financial analyst, or a level-headed friend who isn't emotionally invested in the situation.
3. **Keep a Money Journal** Write down what you're feeling about money and decisions you're considering. You may notice emotional patterns. Just naming the emotion can lower its intensity and keep it from hijacking your judgment.
4. **Create a Post-Divorce Spending Plan** Call it a budget if you want, but this isn't about restricting you. It's about building stability. Factor in your new income, housing, legal costs, and lifestyle shifts.
5. **Reframe the Narrative** Every dollar decision is a vote for the life you

want next. That vacation or new car might feel good for a weekend, but the peace of mind from a strong savings account will last longer.

Pros and Cons of Common Emotional Financial Responses

Keeping the House: **Pros**: Stability for kids, emotional comfort, familiar surroundings. **Cons**: High maintenance costs, possible mortgage imbalance, eats into retirement or savings.

Taking the Retirement Accounts in Exchange for the House: **Pros**: Keeps family home, sentimental value. **Cons**: Misses out on compound growth, risks future liquidity problems, higher tax burdens.

Not Asking for Spousal Support to "Keep the Peace": **Pros**: Less conflict in short term. **Cons**: Sacrifices financial security, can breed resentment, may not be reversible.

Giving More Than Required to Avoid Guilt: **Pros**: Eases emotional burden temporarily. **Cons**: Weakens your position, creates expectation, risks long-term instability.

Action Steps to Protect Yourself Financially During Emotional Highs

- Identify one financial decision you're tempted to make from emotion right now. Hit pause. Write it down. Revisit it in 72 hours with a clear head.
- Create a simple support system: a financial advisor, therapist, and one trusted friend. You need all three during this time.
- Set spending alerts or limits on your bank app to help you check yourself in real time.
- Automate essentials: mortgage/rent, car, utilities, minimum debt payments. Remove daily decision-making from your emotional bandwidth.
- Block time weekly to check in with your money. Make it a ritual—light a candle, pour coffee, make it a moment of calm.
- Create an "emergency pause phrase" for yourself. Something like, "This can wait. Peace costs less than regret."

Reclaiming Power Through Financial Clarity

Making smart money moves isn't about being perfect. It's about being present. About noticing when your emotions want to take the wheel and choosing instead to drive with intention.

Your ex doesn't control your financial future. Your past mistakes don't define your worth. Your current fear doesn't cancel your future power.

Every calm financial choice is a step toward the life you're building. A life rooted in strength, not survival.

So let yourself grieve. Let yourself feel. Then let your next financial move come from your vision, not your pain.

You got this.

And when it feels too hard, remember: every page of this book is here to walk with you, steady your hands, and remind you what's possible when you take your money seriously—because you're taking yourself seriously.

This is your next chapter. Let's write it with clarity and confidence.

Chapter 7: Keeping the Lights On – Budgeting Through the Process

Let's talk about one of the most critical survival skills during divorce: keeping your financial lights on—literally and metaphorically.

In the thick of separation, your world feels like it's been turned upside down. You may be navigating a new home, child custody transitions, legal bills, emotional exhaustion, and the challenge of doing it all with a single income. That's why budgeting isn't just about math right now. It's about survival, stability, and slowly rebuilding control.

This chapter is here to be your flashlight in that financial fog. We'll walk through what budgeting looks like in real-time, when your life is in transition. You don't need to have it all figured out—you just need a system that helps you see clearly and make empowered choices.

Why Budgeting Is More Critical Now Than Ever

You might have budgeted before. Maybe you even managed the money in your household before the divorce. But budgeting after or during divorce is different.

There are new expenses. New income realities. New fears. New goals. And all of that requires a new strategy.

Budgeting is how you:

- Keep the utilities on
- Feed your children
- Protect your credit

- Avoid debt traps
- Save for your future
- Rebuild peace of mind

In the early days, it may feel like you're doing little more than treading water. That's okay. The goal is to create breathing room. To understand what's coming in, what's going out, and how to stretch and structure your resources.

Start With What You Know

Before you start projecting or planning, list your current, *known* financial numbers. Don't guess. Don't round. Pull the actual data.

Write down:

- Monthly net income (after taxes)
- Child support or spousal support received (or paid)
- Housing expenses: mortgage or rent
- Utilities: electric, water, gas, internet, phone
- Transportation: car payment, gas, insurance, rideshare
- Groceries and household supplies
- Insurance premiums
- Minimum debt payments
- Child-related costs: daycare, school fees, clothes, activities

Gather your bank statements, credit card bills, and pay stubs. Then build a real-world snapshot of your monthly money life.

Embrace Zero-Based Budgeting

Zero-based budgeting means every dollar you make gets a job. You don't just guess what's left over. You assign your money to specific categories until there's nothing unaccounted for.

This works especially well when money feels tight, because it helps prevent emotional overspending and hidden leaks.

Steps:

1. Add up all sources of income.
2. List all categories of expenses.
3. Subtract fixed expenses first.
4. Assign a job to every remaining dollar: savings, debt payments, groceries, personal care.
5. The goal is for income minus expenses to equal $0.

You're not *spending* every dollar. You're giving each one a mission.

Track Every Dollar

Now's not the time for fuzzy memory. Use a budgeting app, spreadsheet, or paper journal to track every expense.

Start with a 30-day challenge: write down every dollar spent.

You'll likely be shocked at how much goes to takeout, subscriptions, or things you didn't even consciously choose.

Awareness is everything. It's the difference between feeling broke and realizing you actually had control all along—you just weren't watching.

Cut, Slash, Trim – Without Shame

If your budget doesn't balance, or your income barely covers the basics, it's time to make some changes.

Start with non-essentials:

- Subscriptions (streaming, apps, boxes)
- Dining out and convenience foods
- Gym memberships you don't use
- High cell phone or cable bills

Then look at:

- Groceries (shop with a list, compare prices, avoid waste)
- Utilities (turn down heat, reduce water use, unplug devices)
- Insurance (call for better rates)

This isn't forever. It's a temporary austerity move to get you through the chaos. Don't associate frugality with failure. Associate it with power.

Protect the Essentials First

When things get really tight, use the "Four Walls" approach:

1. Shelter (rent/mortgage)
2. Utilities (heat, water, basic phone)
3. Food
4. Transportation

These come before debt payments. Before birthday gifts. Before guilt purchases.

Credit card companies can wait. Your kids can't.

Emotional Spending: Watch for Triggers

Divorce is an emotional landmine. You're grieving, healing, possibly parenting alone, and dealing with identity shifts. Spending can become a coping mechanism.

Common triggers:

- Loneliness
- Guilt with your kids
- Wanting to keep up appearances
- Revenge or validation spending

Solutions:

- Build in small pleasures you budget for
- Use cash for emotional spending triggers
- Call a friend instead of online shopping
- Journal before major purchases

Income Boosters

Sometimes there's no more room to cut. That's when you increase your income.

Ideas:

- Freelance or side hustle (writing, tutoring, graphic design)
- Sell unused items (clothes, electronics, furniture)
- Take on part-time work
- Ask for a raise or additional hours

Remember, this is about breathing room, not burnout. One extra $200/month can change everything.

Building a Crisis Budget vs. a Recovery Budget

Crisis Budget: bare minimum, survive-now budget. No fluff. Just the essentials and immediate needs.

Recovery Budget: slow rebuild, includes savings, debt repayment, and some joy.

Know which one you're in. Accept it without judgment. And have a plan to graduate from one to the next.

Pros and Cons of Budgeting Tools

Apps (e.g., YNAB, EveryDollar, Mint) Pros:

- Easy to use
- Categorization built-in
- Real-time alerts

Cons:

- Learning curve
- Subscription fees
- Can feel impersonal

Spreadsheets (Excel, Google Sheets) Pros:

- Fully customizable
- No extra cost

Cons:

- Requires setup
- More manual tracking

Pen-and-Paper Budgeting Pros:

- Deep mindfulness
- Helps with discipline

Cons:

- Slower updates
- Easier to make errors

Action Steps

1. List all your sources of income.
2. Identify your fixed monthly expenses.
3. Track every expense for 30 days.
4. Cut or reduce non-essentials.
5. Build a zero-based budget.
6. Choose and use a tracking method.
7. Establish a crisis vs. recovery plan.
8. Build your "Four Walls" plan.
9. Watch for emotional spending habits.
10. Explore side income ideas.

Reflection

You don't have to be a financial expert to make a budget.

You just have to care about your future more than your momentary comfort.

You can do this. Even if it feels slow. Even if you mess up. Even if the math doesn't feel pretty.

A good budget is a promise. It's you saying to yourself: I'm not giving up. I'm building again. I'm keeping the lights on until the sun comes back out.

You're not alone. You're not behind. And you are absolutely strong enough to make it through this part, one dollar—and one decision—at a time.

Chapter 8: Temporary Orders, Alimony, and Spousal Support Basics

Let's be honest—when you're going through a divorce, there's a lot coming at you fast. One of the biggest areas that can knock you off balance is money. Specifically, the question of how the bills are going to get paid during the divorce, and what happens financially after it's all finalized. This chapter is going to walk you through the basics of temporary orders, alimony, and spousal support so you can understand your options, protect yourself, and create a plan you can live with—literally.

What Are Temporary Orders?

Think of temporary orders like a financial timeout while the divorce plays out. These are short-term legal decisions made by the court that help manage immediate financial responsibilities until the final divorce agreement is in place.

They can cover things like:

- Who stays in the house
- Who pays the mortgage or rent
- Who covers which bills
- Temporary child support or custody arrangements
- Temporary spousal support

Temporary orders are usually requested early in the divorce process. They provide some stability and structure during what is usually a very emotional and uncertain time.

Why Temporary Orders Matter

Temporary orders aren't just about convenience. They can set the tone for the rest of your divorce. Judges often look at what was ordered temporarily when deciding the final arrangements.

So if your temporary orders have you paying all the household bills and supporting your spouse, don't assume it's just for now. It could become the long-term expectation unless you speak up.

Action Steps: Preparing for Temporary Orders

- **Gather financial documents**: Show what you earn, what you owe, and what you spend.
- **Create a list of current bills and responsibilities**: Rent, utilities, childcare, insurance, groceries—lay it all out.
- **Think about what's fair and what you need**: Don't overpromise or agree to something you can't sustain.

Bring this information to your attorney or mediator. These documents are your receipts, your evidence, your protection.

Understanding Alimony and Spousal Support

Alimony and spousal support refer to the same concept: one spouse financially supporting the other after divorce. The purpose is to help the lower-earning or non-earning spouse maintain a reasonable standard of living after the marriage ends.

There are a few types:

- **Temporary alimony**: Paid while the divorce is still happening (this is part of those temporary orders).
- **Rehabilitative alimony**: Short-term support to help a spouse get back on their feet (get a job, finish school, etc.).
- **Permanent alimony**: Less common today, but awarded when one spouse may never be able to be self-supporting due to age, health, or long-term absence from the workforce.
- **Lump sum alimony**: One-time payment instead of monthly checks.

How Is Alimony Decided?

Alimony isn't guaranteed. It's based on a variety of factors, which can include:

- Length of the marriage
- Each spouse's income and earning potential
- Contributions to the marriage (including homemaking and child-rearing)
- Age and health of both parties
- Standard of living during the marriage
- Education and job skills of each spouse

Pros and Cons of Alimony

Pros (for recipient):

- Financial stability
- Time to build independence

Cons (for recipient):

- Can end if the payer loses their job or retires
- May be taxable (depends on the agreement and current tax law)

Pros (for payer):

- Structured payments
- Possible tax deductions (check with a CPA)

Cons (for payer):

- Financial burden
- Can feel punitive if the relationship ended badly

How to Handle Alimony Emotionally and Strategically

This is one of those parts of divorce where emotions run high. If you're paying, it may feel like a punishment. If you're receiving, it may feel like a lifeline mixed with guilt. Either way, keep your head clear.

Remind yourself:

- Alimony is not a reward or a punishment. It's a financial tool.
- If you're receiving it, use it to build toward independence.
- If you're paying it, factor it into your new budget and focus on your fresh start.

Action Steps: Navigating Alimony

- **Get clear on your income and expenses.** You need to know your numbers.
- **Work with a financial planner or advisor.** They can help you model scenarios.
- **If you're negotiating, ask for what you need—not what you think is "fair."** Fair is subjective. You need realistic numbers.
- **Consider a lump sum if you want closure and can afford it.** But understand the risks.

Common Myths About Alimony

"Only women get alimony." False. Either spouse can receive support depending on the financial dynamic.

"It lasts forever." Rarely. Most alimony is time-limited or can be modified.

"If I remarry, I still get alimony." Usually not. Most alimony agreements end if the recipient remarries or cohabitates.

Final Thoughts: Advocate for Yourself

If you take nothing else from this chapter, take this: you are allowed to advocate for your financial future. Whether you're asking for support or being asked to pay it, this is about stability, not revenge. It's about giving both parties a fair chance to start over.

Don't let shame, guilt, or pride keep you from negotiating what you need. And don't let anger push you into agreeing to something you can't afford.

Ask questions. Run the numbers. Speak up.

You are not being greedy. You are being responsible.

And responsibility is the first step toward healing, rebuilding, and living well again.

Part 2: The Financial Fallout – Navigating the Divorce Process

This part of the book is all about managing the emotional and financial turbulence that often hits during the actual divorce proceedings. When papers are filed and emotions are raw, it can feel like your whole world is being split in half—your home, your routines, your future plans, and yes, your finances. This section is designed to guide you through that storm with clarity, confidence, and control.

We'll start by helping you assemble the right team—the lawyer who listens, the mediator who sees both sides, the advisor who's thinking long-term while you're just trying to make it through today. From there, we'll walk you through essential topics like temporary orders, spousal support, and what to do if kids are involved—from custody to child support to co-parenting budgets.

You'll also learn how to build and manage a budget during a time when your income may feel unpredictable and your expenses are climbing fast. And because divorce isn't just a legal process—it's an emotional one—we'll talk about how to avoid money decisions driven by grief, anger, or fear. Selling the house, fighting over accounts, agreeing to things just to "get it over with"—these are traps that can set you back for years. You'll learn how to avoid them.

By the end of Part 2, you'll not only understand the systems and structures of the divorce process, but you'll also have tools to stay grounded in what matters most: protecting your financial health, your emotional peace, and your path forward. This isn't just about surviving—it's about navigating wisely so you can rebuild stronger.

Chapter 9: Divorce and Your Net Worth – What's at Stake

Let's take a breath before we dive in.

Because this one? This one hits deep.

After all the arguments, the late-night tears, the legal back-and-forth—you're now being asked to divide not just a life, but everything that came with it. Assets. Debts. Retirement accounts. Credit cards. Homes. Cars. Business interests. Even that $75 coffee table you bought when you first moved in together.

It's overwhelming. It's emotional. But it's also essential.

This chapter is about getting clear on what's at stake financially so that you can protect your future—not just react to the pain of the past.

Your net worth is more than just a number. It's the sum of what you own minus what you owe. And in divorce, it becomes the foundation of every negotiation and legal decision that follows. So let's unpack what it really means, how to calculate it, and how to walk through this process with clarity, confidence, and care.

What Is Net Worth—and Why It Matters in Divorce

Net worth is like your financial report card. It's a snapshot of your current financial health and the result of every decision, investment, debt, and expense made over the years.

It's calculated like this:

Net Worth = Total Assets – Total Liabilities

Assets are everything you own that has value—cash, property, cars, retirement accounts, stocks, jewelry, businesses.

Liabilities are what you owe—credit cards, student loans, mortgages, auto loans, personal loans, medical bills.

When you subtract your debts from your assets, you get your net worth.

But in a divorce, your net worth isn't just yours. It's part of the "marital estate." And that's what gets divided.

Marital vs. Separate Property: What's What

Not everything gets split 50/50 in a divorce. Depending on your state and circumstances, the law typically distinguishes between:

- **Marital Property:** Assets and debts acquired during the marriage—joint bank accounts, the home you bought together, retirement contributions made while married, vehicles, and debts in both names.
- **Separate Property:** Anything you owned before the marriage, inherited solely, or were gifted individually—like grandma's diamond bracelet or a trust fund from your aunt.

But here's where it gets tricky: separate property can become marital property over time, depending on how it was used. For example:

- If you inherited money but put it in a joint bank account = possibly marital
- If you owned a house before marriage but added your spouse to the deed = possibly marital
- If you received a personal injury settlement during marriage = depends on the type of damages

So before you assume anything is "off-limits," gather documentation. Because what matters most isn't just what you think is yours—it's what you can prove.

Chapter 10: Dividing the House – Should You Stay or Sell?

When you're going through a divorce, few decisions carry as much emotional and financial weight as the question: what should happen to the house? For many couples, the marital home represents more than just real estate. It's where holidays were hosted, kids were raised, arguments happened, and healing began. It's the photo album of your shared life, and now you're being asked whether to stay in it or walk away.

This chapter isn't about telling you what to do—it's about helping you explore what makes sense for *you*. Whether you're leaning toward keeping the house or considering selling it and starting fresh, we want you to walk away from this chapter feeling like you made a decision with both your head and your heart.

Understanding the Emotional Attachment

Let's start here, because it's real. Letting go of a home can feel like letting go of a whole chapter of your life. And in some ways, it is.

You might feel a strong desire to hold onto the house to keep things stable for the kids. Maybe you're afraid of the unknown, of starting over in a new place. Or maybe, deep down, you just want to "win" the house because it feels like a symbol of your identity or what you deserve.

These emotions are valid. But they shouldn't be the only thing driving your decision. The goal is to weigh the emotional pull with the practical realities—because the wrong decision can cost you more than money.

The Financial Reality of Keeping the House

On paper, keeping the house might seem like the simpler route. You stay put, the kids stay in the same schools, the routine stays the same.

But let's dig a little deeper.

- **Can you afford the mortgage on your own?**
- **Will your income support maintenance, repairs, taxes, and insurance?**
- **Are you buying your spouse out, and if so, how?**
- **Are you prepared for the cost of refinancing the mortgage in your name alone?**

Owning a home is expensive. If your financial situation is shifting significantly post-divorce, the house might become a financial burden instead of a haven.

Pros of Keeping the House

- Stability for children
- Emotional continuity
- Potential appreciation in property value
- Ability to avoid the hassle of moving

Cons of Keeping the House

- High ongoing costs
- Trapped equity
- Pressure to refinance or buy out your ex
- Emotional strain of living in a space filled with past memories

The Logistics of Selling the House

Sometimes, selling is the cleanest path. It turns a shared asset into liquid cash. You and your ex can split the proceeds, pay off shared debts, and start new chapters without the shadow of the shared home looming over you.

But selling also comes with challenges:

- Timing the sale for the market
- Prepping the house for listing
- Negotiating who pays for repairs or staging
- Deciding how to split proceeds

And if kids are involved, you'll have to decide how to manage the transition with minimal disruption.

Pros of Selling the House

- Clean financial break
- Shared profits
- Opportunity for fresh start
- Less emotional baggage

Cons of Selling the House

- Moving logistics
- Potential disruption for children
- Market uncertainty
- Emotional impact of leaving family home

Questions to Ask Before You Decide

- What will my income look like post-divorce?
- Do I want to remain in this city or neighborhood long-term?
- Will I qualify to refinance the mortgage alone?
- What will housing costs look like if I move?
- Is this decision based on logic or emotion?

Action Steps: If You Decide to Keep the House

1. **Refinance in Your Name**: Contact lenders to see if you qualify based on your income and credit.
2. **Calculate True Costs**: Factor in taxes, maintenance, insurance, and unexpected repairs.
3. **Update Title and Deed**: Ensure the deed reflects your name only, even if your ex's name is off the loan.
4. **Consult a Financial Advisor**: Determine if this is sustainable given your long-term goals.

Action Steps: If You Decide to Sell the House

1. **Agree on a Timeline**: Set realistic expectations with your ex-spouse.
2. **Hire a Realtor**: Choose someone who understands divorce sales.
3. **Discuss Proceeds Split**: Will it be 50/50 or based on another agreement?
4. **Plan Your Next Living Arrangement**: Know where you're going before the house sells.

If You're Undecided: The Nesting Option

Some couples choose to co-own the house temporarily. The kids stay put, and the parents alternate living in the house during their custodial time.

This can be a good transitional strategy but requires:

- High communication and cooperation
- Clear boundaries about finances
- A written agreement for exit strategy

Tax Considerations

- If you sell and make a profit, you may owe capital gains tax. But if you lived there for 2 of the last 5 years, you may qualify for an exclusion ($250,000 single / $500,000 married).

- Mortgage interest deductions change if you refinance solo.

Final Thoughts: Peace of Mind Over Square Footage

A home is a powerful thing. But don't confuse its walls for your worth. Whether you keep it, sell it, or walk away entirely—what matters most is your peace, stability, and forward motion.

There is no "right" choice here. Just the one that aligns best with your next chapter.

Sometimes freedom is worth more than familiarity.

Sometimes a smaller house means a bigger life.

Sometimes, moving forward starts with letting go.

Let your decision be one rooted in clarity, not confusion. And remember: wherever you go next, *you* are what makes it home.

Chapter 11: Retirement Accounts, IRAs, and QDROs Explained

When a marriage ends, everything feels like it's up in the air—your identity, your routine, your emotions, and yes, your money. One of the most overlooked and often misunderstood pieces of the financial puzzle in divorce is retirement savings. This chapter is going to break it all down for you: what accounts matter, how they're divided, and how to make sure you protect your future while you navigate your present.

Let's take a deep breath, sit down at the kitchen table together, and get into it. No judgment, no jargon. Just clarity and calm.

Retirement Accounts: What They Are and Why They Matter

Retirement accounts are savings vehicles designed to help you accumulate money for your later years. In the context of divorce, they're not just about the future—they're a big part of what gets divided.

Common types of retirement accounts include:

- **401(k):** Offered through an employer. Often includes matching contributions.
- **403(b):** Similar to a 401(k), but for employees of schools, nonprofits, and some government organizations.
- **Traditional IRA (Individual Retirement Account):** You contribute

pre-tax money. Taxes come out when you withdraw.

- **Roth IRA:** You contribute after-tax money. Withdrawals are usually tax-free.
- **Pensions:** Employer-sponsored plans that pay a fixed benefit in retirement.

If your ex had a job with any of these accounts while you were married, that retirement money is typically considered marital property—even if your name isn't on the account.

What Gets Divided: Marital vs. Separate Property

Let's clarify one thing: not all of your ex's retirement is yours to claim, and not all of yours is theirs. The key factor is **when the money was earned**.

- **Marital property:** Any retirement money contributed during the marriage (regardless of whose name is on it).
- **Separate property:** Retirement money earned **before** the marriage or after a legal separation or divorce decree.

This is why gathering records is so important. You'll need account statements that show balances at the time of marriage and at the time of divorce to determine the "marital portion."

Meet the QDRO: Your Ticket to a Fair Split

If you're splitting a 401(k) or pension, you'll likely need a **Qualified Domestic Relations Order**, or **QDRO** (pronounced "kwah-dro" or "cue-dro").

A QDRO is a court order that tells the retirement plan administrator to divide the account and pay a portion to an alternate payee (that could be you).

Without a QDRO, the plan won't honor your right to a share of the retirement benefits—even if your divorce decree says you should get them.

Key QDRO Facts:

- Applies only to qualified plans (401(k)s and pensions, not IRAs).
- Must be drafted carefully to avoid tax penalties.
- Usually requires a lawyer or QDRO specialist to prepare.

What About IRAs?

IRAs are a little different. You don't need a QDRO to divide an IRA, but you do need to be careful.

If the transfer isn't handled correctly, you could owe taxes and penalties.

To divide an IRA in a divorce:

- It must be spelled out clearly in the divorce decree.
- The transfer should be a **trustee-to-trustee** transfer, not a withdrawal and deposit.

Pro tip: Don't touch the money yourself. Let the institutions handle it. That way, you avoid triggering income taxes or a 10% early withdrawal penalty.

Pros and Cons of Accepting Retirement Assets in Divorce

Pros:

- Can provide long-term financial security.
- Often significant in value.
- Potential for tax-deferred growth.

Cons:

- You can't use them right away without penalties.

- Market value may fluctuate.
- You may owe taxes on withdrawals, depending on the account type.

Make sure you balance your needs. If you need cash now, taking the house and giving up retirement assets may seem attractive—but fast forward 20 years, and you may wish you had done the opposite.

Action Steps: What To Do Next

1. **Inventory All Retirement Accounts**

- Yours and your ex's.
- Include type, value, and date of contributions.

1. **Get Statements and Documents**

- Go back to the year you were married.
- Request summary plan descriptions (SPDs) if applicable.

1. **Consult a Financial or Legal Expert**

- You may need a divorce financial planner or attorney who understands QDROs.

1. **Determine What Needs a QDRO**

- For 401(k)s and pensions only.
- IRAs require only a divorce decree.

1. **Consider Tax Implications**

- Talk to a tax advisor.
- Remember: Roth money is taxed up front, traditional money later.

1. **Weigh Your Options**

- Do you want current value (home equity) or future value (retirement)?
- Think long-term, not just survival mode.

1. **Update Your Own Retirement Plan**

- Open your own IRA if you haven't already.
- Start contributing immediately—even small amounts help.

Rebuilding Your Retirement Life

Divorce may have shaken your financial future, but it doesn't mean you won't have one. In fact, this can be the moment when you take full ownership of your wealth and begin to build on your own terms.

- Contribute what you can, when you can.
- Automate contributions to make it easier.
- Revisit your strategy annually.
- Don't be afraid to ask for help.

Final Reflection

You are not behind. You are not broken. You are in a transition.

And while it might feel unfair that something your partner built while you held the household together now requires legal paperwork just to access, know this: your contributions matter. Your future matters. And protecting your share of the retirement pie isn't greedy—it's responsible.

Whether you're 30 or 60, the best time to start building your new financial life is now. Not with fear, not with guilt, but with clarity, calm, and the confidence that you deserve a future full of freedom, rest, and choice.

You got this. Let's keep going.

Chapter 12: Health Insurance, Life Insurance, and Estate Docs in Transition

When the dust settles after divorce, one of the most overlooked but critical aspects of rebuilding your financial life is insurance and estate planning. These tools aren't just about paperwork or policies—they're about protection, peace of mind, and planning for what comes next. Whether you're a parent navigating new responsibilities, someone facing an unexpected shift in coverage, or simply trying to get your footing again, this chapter walks you through how to manage your health insurance, life insurance, and estate documents with clarity and confidence.

Let's start with what often feels the most immediate: health insurance.

HEALTH INSURANCE: WHAT NOW?

Divorce often triggers an automatic change in health insurance eligibility. If you were on your spouse's plan, you may lose that coverage once the divorce is finalized. And if your children were on a shared plan, you'll need to determine who will carry coverage and how medical expenses will be split moving forward.

Options for Health Insurance:

1. COBRA: This federal law allows you to stay on your ex-spouse's employer plan for up to 36 months, but you pay the full premium plus a 2% administrative fee. It's a good short-term option if you're in between jobs or need continuity of care.

2. Pros:

- Immediate continuation of coverage
- No need to switch doctors or plans

1. Cons:

- Often expensive without employer subsidy
- Only temporary

1. Your Own Employer: If you work, ask HR about enrolling in your company's plan. Divorce is considered a qualifying event, which means you don't have to wait for open enrollment.
2. The Marketplace (Healthcare.gov): Depending on your income, you may qualify for subsidies or Medicaid. This is especially useful if your divorce significantly alters your financial situation.

Action Steps:

- Call your current insurance provider and find out when your coverage ends.
- Explore all three options above and compare premiums, deductibles, and coverage levels.
- Don't let yourself go uninsured. Medical debt is one of the most common causes of financial hardship.

LIFE INSURANCE: NEW PRIORITIES, NEW BENEFICIARIES

Life insurance isn't just about protecting your former partner in case something happens to you—it's about protecting the people who rely on you now. That might be your kids, your aging parents, or even yourself.

Types of Life Insurance:

- Term Life: Covers you for a set number of years (usually 10, 20, or 30).

It's the most affordable and straightforward option.

- Whole Life: A permanent policy that also builds cash value. More expensive, but includes an investment component.
- Universal Life: A flexible policy with adjustable premiums and benefits, often used for estate planning.

If you already have life insurance, update your beneficiaries immediately. Many people forget this, and it results in benefits going to ex-spouses instead of children, siblings, or new partners.

Pros and Cons of Updating Your Policy:

Pros:

- Ensures your wishes are respected
- Reflects your new reality

Cons:

- May require underwriting again if replacing old policy
- Emotional resistance (you may feel guilty removing your ex)

Action Steps:

- Review existing policies: type, term, beneficiaries, and premium.
- Decide if you need new or additional coverage.
- Update beneficiaries.
- If children are involved, consider setting up a trust to receive life insurance proceeds, with a trusted adult as trustee.

ESTATE DOCUMENTS: POWER, CONTROL, AND PEACE

Your will, power of attorney, and healthcare directives likely include your ex-spouse. That needs to change.

Key Documents to Update:

- Will: Designate new heirs and guardians for children, if needed.
- Durable Power of Attorney: Who will make financial decisions for you if you're incapacitated?
- Healthcare Proxy: Who will make medical decisions on your behalf?
- Living Will: What are your wishes for end-of-life care?
- Trusts: If you had a joint trust, consult an estate attorney about dissolving it or setting up individual trusts.

Why These Updates Matter:

- Avoid confusion and conflict
- Prevent your ex-spouse from having unintended control
- Protect your kids and assets

Empowering Mindset: You're not just protecting what you have now; you're building something better. These documents are your voice in moments when you might not be able to speak.

Action Steps:

- Schedule an appointment with an estate planning attorney.
- Make a list of who you trust in various roles (executor, power of attorney, guardian).
- Ensure all documents align with your current financial and personal life.

COORDINATING IT ALL

Now that you've reviewed health insurance, life insurance, and estate documents individually, it's time to make sure they work together.

Check for these alignment issues:

- Do your life insurance beneficiaries match the intentions in your will?
- If you named your new partner in one place, did you forget to update another?

- If your ex is co-parenting, do you have language in your will about guardianship or financial management?

The Power of an Annual Review: Your life will keep evolving. Review these documents every year or after major life changes—job moves, remarriage, illness, or children aging into adulthood.

Closing Reflection: You've come a long way. Maybe this chapter brought up some fears, some questions, or some painful reminders. That's okay. Take a deep breath. Every form you fill out, every name you update, every policy you review—it's a step toward security, self-determination, and stability.

You are not the same person you were before the divorce. You're wiser. Stronger. And more in control than you realize.

Don't let the paperwork intimidate you. It's just the structure around a new life you're building—brick by brick, page by page, plan by plan.

And if no one else has told you lately: You're doing a good job.

Chapter 13: Credit Scores and Joint Debt – What to Know and What to Do

Let's take a deep breath.

Because if you're reading this chapter, it means you're standing at a financial crossroads, probably in the middle of the storm that comes with divorce. And while credit and debt may not be the most emotional parts of divorce, they can absolutely affect how long it takes you to find your financial peace again.

This chapter is your no-fluff, sit-down conversation about what credit scores really mean after divorce, what to do with joint debt, and how to start rebuilding your financial foundation from the ground up. We're going to take all the fear, confusion, and overwhelm around this topic and turn it into a clear, empowering action plan.

Why Credit Matters (Even More After Divorce)

Let's start with this truth: Your credit score is not your worth. But it is a powerful financial tool. It impacts everything from renting a new apartment, to refinancing your car, to opening a new credit card in your name alone.

After divorce, your credit becomes even more important because you're shifting from shared finances to independence. That means your name, your score, your accounts, your responsibility. There's freedom in that, but also some risk—especially if your credit was tied up in joint debt, or if your former spouse didn't manage their side well.

Understanding Your Credit Score

Your credit score is a three-digit number ranging from 300 to 850 that reflects how well you manage debt. It's made up of:

- **Payment history (35%)**: Do you pay your bills on time?
- **Amounts owed (30%)**: How much of your available credit are you using?
- **Length of credit history (15%)**: How long have your accounts been open?
- **New credit (10%)**: Have you applied for credit recently?
- **Credit mix (10%)**: Do you have a variety of accounts (credit cards, mortgage, student loans, etc.)?

Why is this important? Because divorce can shake every one of these factors. If a joint account goes unpaid, it can ding both credit reports. If you close old accounts out of frustration or fear, you shorten your credit history. If you max out a card to cover legal fees, your usage spikes.

Let's talk about how to protect yourself.

Start With Your Credit Report

Before you make any moves, get a copy of your credit reports from all three bureaus: Experian, Equifax, and TransUnion.

Look for:

- Joint accounts still open
- Missed payments or late fees
- Accounts you didn't know were in your name
- Old addresses, phone numbers, or errors

Action Step: Visit annualcreditreport.com and request all three reports. Review every line. Highlight anything that looks off.

Separate What You Can – Joint Debt Basics

Joint accounts are exactly what they sound like: both names, both responsibilities. And even if your divorce decree says your ex is responsible for a certain debt, that doesn't mean the creditor agrees. If your name is on the account, you're legally responsible for the debt—period.

Types of joint debt to look for:

- Joint credit cards
- Co-signed loans (car, student, personal)
- Mortgages or home equity loans

Here's what you need to know:

- **You can request to be removed** from some accounts (like credit cards), but both parties may have to agree.
- **Refinancing** might be necessary to remove one name from a loan or mortgage.
- **Closing the account** may protect your credit, but could also hurt your score temporarily.

Pros:

- Protects your credit if your ex is financially unstable
- Gives you a clean slate

Cons:

- May reduce your available credit
- Could increase your usage ratio
- Might not be possible if your ex won't cooperate

Action Step: Make a list of all joint debts. Contact each lender to understand your options for removal, closure, or refinancing.

Build New Credit in Your Name Alone

This is your next play. Even if your credit took a hit during the divorce, rebuilding is absolutely possible. Here's how you start:

- Apply for a secured credit card (uses a deposit to back your limit)
- Keep balances low and pay in full monthly
- Avoid late payments at all costs
- Don't open too many new accounts at once

You're not just building a score. You're building trust with future lenders—and with yourself.

Protecting Yourself From Credit Damage That's Not Yours

Let's be real. Not every divorce ends with both people doing the right thing.

If your ex racks up charges on a joint card, misses payments, or defaults on a loan, it can hurt your score—even if you're not the one using the account.

That's why it's critical to:

- Freeze joint cards (stop new charges)
- Close or refinance joint accounts as soon as possible
- Put written agreements in place about who pays what (and document everything)

And if damage has already been done?

- Contact the creditor and dispute the charge
- Provide a copy of your divorce decree
- Ask for a goodwill adjustment if appropriate

It may not be fair, but it is fixable.

The Role of Authorized Users

Many couples add each other as authorized users on credit cards. That can help build credit when things are good—but can destroy it when things go bad.

If you're an authorized user on your ex's card:

- You're not legally responsible for the debt
- But if they miss payments, it can still hurt your credit

Action Step: Remove yourself as an authorized user on any card that doesn't belong to you. Call the issuer directly.

What About Student Loans?

If you co-signed for your ex's student loan, you're still on the hook. Same with Parent PLUS loans. The only way to get off is through refinance or full payoff. Talk to a financial advisor or student loan expert about your options.

Managing the Emotional Side of Credit

Credit feels cold and impersonal, but divorce is not. There's emotion tied to every dollar and every decision. You might feel embarrassed about your score, frustrated by your ex, or defeated by how much work there is to do.

That's okay. Feel those things. Then let's take one small step forward.

Every payment made on time is a win. Every joint account closed is a fresh start. Every point your score climbs is a reminder: You're rebuilding, not breaking.

Tools to Use

- Credit Karma or Credit Sesame for free score tracking
- Experian Boost to add utility bills or rent to your credit history
- NerdWallet or Mint for managing debt repayment
- Annualcreditreport.com for your full reports

Wrap-Up: You Are Not Your Score

Let's close with this: Divorce might shake your finances, but it doesn't define your financial future.

Your credit score is a snapshot, not a sentence. It's something you can influence, improve, and protect with consistent action. You don't need to be perfect. You just need to be committed.

So check your reports. Make your plan. Set your boundaries with debt.

And keep showing up for your financial future like it matters—because it does.

The road ahead may not be easy, but it will absolutely be worth it. This chapter is the beginning of your comeback. Keep going.

Chapter 14: Taxes and Divorce – Filing Status, Deductions, and Dependents

Divorce changes a lot more than just your relationship status. It touches your identity, your schedule, your finances—and yes, your taxes. And while that might not sound exciting, understanding how taxes work post-divorce is one of the most empowering financial steps you can take. Because taxes affect your refund, your paycheck, your child support, and your ability to rebuild after a life shake-up.

So let's walk through this together. Not with IRS jargon or financial lingo that makes your eyes glaze over. But like we're sitting at your kitchen table, coffee in hand, helping you sort out what this all means.

The Emotional Weight Behind the Numbers

Let's be real for a moment.

Taxes after divorce aren't just numbers on a page. They can trigger all kinds of feelings:

- "Am I doing this right?"
- "Is this going to screw up my refund?"
- "Why does it feel like they're winning even here?"

This chapter is here to help you turn that confusion and stress into clarity and power. Because once you understand the rules, you can play the game wisely.

First Things First: Filing Status

Your filing status determines how much tax you owe, your standard deduction, and even your eligibility for credits. Here are your main options:

Married Filing Jointly (MFJ)

This is the most common filing status for married couples. If you're still legally married as of **December 31** of the tax year, the IRS considers you married for the whole year.

Married Filing Separately (MFS)

Still married but living apart? You may choose to file separately. But beware—this often results in **higher taxes** and fewer deductions.

Head of Household (HOH)

This is a **game-changer** if you qualify. It comes with a higher standard deduction and lower tax brackets.

To qualify for Head of Household, you must:

- Be unmarried (or considered unmarried) on the last day of the year
- Have paid more than half the cost of keeping up a home
- Have a qualifying child or dependent live with you for more than half the year

Single

If you don't meet the criteria for HOH and you're legally divorced or separated by December 31, you'll file as Single.

The Pros and Cons of Filing Options

Head of Household

- Pros: Lower taxes, higher deductions

- Cons: Must meet the dependency and household cost rules

Single

- Pros: Simpler if you have no dependents
- Cons: Higher tax rates than HOH

Married Filing Separately

- Pros: Can protect yourself from a spouse's tax issues
- Cons: Lose out on credits like the Earned Income Credit

Action Step:

- **Check your calendar.** Your marital status on **December 31** determines your tax status.
- **Talk to a tax pro** if you're unsure which status fits your situation.

Child Support and Taxes

Child support is **not taxable income**. It doesn't count as income to the parent receiving it, and it's not deductible for the parent paying it.

This is a big surprise for a lot of folks. If you're paying $1,000/month in child support, that money is **after-tax** dollars—meaning you pay taxes on it and then send it.

On the flip side, if you're receiving child support, you don't report it on your taxes.

Who Gets to Claim the Kids?

This is where things get sticky.

Claiming a child as a dependent can unlock several valuable tax benefits:

- Child Tax Credit
- Head of Household status
- Dependent Care Credit
- Earned Income Tax Credit (EITC)

Generally, the custodial parent (the one the child lives with more than 50% of the year) gets to claim the child **unless** there is a written agreement that says otherwise.

You can fill out IRS Form 8332 to allow the noncustodial parent to claim the child. But be careful. This is not something to take lightly. If you sign it, it can have **real financial impact.**

Pros and Cons of Letting the Other Parent Claim the Child

Pros:

- May reduce conflict if both parties agree
- Could be a negotiation point in other financial matters

Cons:

- You lose out on valuable credits
- Once signed, it can be hard to undo retroactively

Action Step:

- **Decide ahead of time** who will claim the child on taxes. Put it in your divorce decree if possible.
- **Don't just alternate years** unless it's part of a larger strategy.

Spousal Support (Alimony) and Taxes

This changed in 2019.

For divorces finalized before January 1, 2019:

- Alimony payments are **tax-deductible** for the payer
- Alimony is **taxable income** for the recipient

For divorces finalized on or after January 1, 2019:

- Alimony is **not deductible** for the payer
- Alimony is **not taxable income** for the recipient

This is huge. If you're negotiating alimony, make sure your expectations reflect current tax law.

Retirement and Investment Taxes

Don't forget: splitting retirement accounts often involves **Qualified Domestic Relations Orders** (QDROs). These let you transfer part of a retirement account **without penalty** during divorce.

But be mindful:

- Distributions from retirement accounts may be **taxable**
- Transferring without a QDRO can lead to **penalties**

Action Step:

- If retirement assets are being divided, make sure a QDRO is in place and executed correctly

Deductions You Might Miss After Divorce

- Mortgage Interest Deduction (if you no longer own the house)
- Married Filing Jointly Standard Deduction (if you're now filing as Single or HOH)
- Child Tax Credit (if you no longer claim your child)

Be ready for this. Your refund may be smaller than you're used to.

Your New Withholding Strategy

If you're working, make sure your **W-4 form** at work reflects your new filing status.

Too many people go through a divorce and forget to update this. Then tax season comes and they owe more than they expected.

Action Step:

- File a new W-4 with your HR department
- Use the IRS Withholding Estimator tool to adjust accordingly

Tax Documents Checklist Post-Divorce

Here are the key docs to gather and update:

- Divorce decree
- Form 8332 (if applicable)
- New W-4
- Last year's tax return
- Custody agreement
- Alimony payment documentation
- Health insurance records (if coverage changed)

Final Thoughts: Taxes Are a Tool, Not a Trap

Look, we get it. After everything you've just gone through, the last thing you want is to get tangled up in tax talk.

But here's the truth: understanding this stuff can **put money back in your pocket.** It can help you rebuild. It can help you breathe again.

Don't try to go it alone. This is one of the areas where investing in a good CPA or tax preparer is worth every penny. Because taxes aren't just about this year. They're about setting up your next chapter with clarity and confidence.

You deserve that.

And you've got this.

Chapter 15: Negotiating a Fair Settlement – What's "Fair" Isn't Always Equal

Let's get something out in the open: fair doesn't always mean equal. And when it comes to divorce settlements, that difference matters. A lot.

When you're going through a separation, especially if emotions are running high, it can be easy to default to what feels "equal"—split everything 50/50 and move on. But that might not be the outcome that truly supports your long-term financial health or reflects the realities of your life, especially if your earning power, caregiving duties, or financial knowledge were different from your partner's during the marriage.

This chapter is about helping you understand what a fair settlement might look like for you—and how to stand up for it. Not aggressively, not vengefully—strategically. With clarity, preparation, and a vision for your future that guides your decisions today.

Understanding the Foundation: What Gets Negotiated

When you go through a divorce, you're essentially unwinding a financial partnership. And just like any business breakup, that means taking stock, assigning value, and figuring out how to move forward. Here are some of the most common assets and financial items that come into play:

- The house (and any other property)
- Retirement accounts (401(k)s, IRAs, pensions)

- Investment accounts and savings
- Business ownership or interests
- Debts (joint or individual)
- Cars and physical assets
- Personal property (jewelry, art, furniture)
- Spousal support (alimony)
- Child support
- Future tax implications of asset division

It's not just what you get—it's what it means for your future. Taking the house might sound like a win, but if it comes with a giant mortgage you can't afford alone, that "win" becomes a financial trap. Keeping retirement funds intact might not help if you need liquid cash to survive. That's why financial literacy is key to negotiating a smart settlement.

Fair vs. Equal: Why 50/50 Can Be Misleading

Equal means everything is split down the middle. Sounds simple. But fair takes into account things like:

- Who stayed home to raise kids
- Who gave up career opportunities for the family
- Who managed the finances or owned more assets
- Differences in future earning potential
- Health issues or caregiving responsibilities

Let's say one partner worked a high-paying job while the other stayed home and raised the kids, cooked meals, managed school schedules, and ran the household. They didn't bring home a paycheck, but their unpaid labor allowed the other partner to climb the career ladder. An equal split might ignore that dynamic. A fair one acknowledges it.

Common Mistakes to Avoid When Negotiating a Divorce Settlement

Letting Emotions Drive Decisions You may want to keep the house because it's familiar. Or fight for every dollar as payback. Or walk away with less just to get it over with. All of those are emotional decisions that may hurt you financially long-term.

Not Valuing Assets Correctly It's easy to assign emotional value to things, but you also need to assign financial value. That antique table? It might have meaning but isn't worth what you think. Meanwhile, your ex's 401(k) could grow to six figures over time.

Forgetting About Taxes Not all money is created equal. Getting $50,000 from a checking account is not the same as getting $50,000 from a pre-tax retirement account. One is yours to spend; the other will be taxed later.

Not Considering Long-Term Impact You might win today's negotiation and lose tomorrow's freedom. Take time to understand how this settlement affects your life 5, 10, 20 years down the road.

Pros and Cons of Different Settlement Approaches

Option 1: Mediation Pros:

- Lower legal costs
- More cooperative
- Faster resolution

Cons:

- Not ideal if there's an imbalance of power
- May not uncover hidden assets
- Less protection if things get contentious

Option 2: Collaborative Divorce Pros:

- Both parties commit to a respectful process
- Uses a team approach (lawyers, coaches, financial specialists)
- Focuses on long-term family wellness

Cons:

- Can be expensive

- If the process breaks down, you start over with new attorneys

Option 3: Traditional Litigation Pros:

- Strong legal protection
- Can force discovery if one spouse is hiding assets

Cons:

- Expensive and time-consuming
- Can increase hostility
- Outcome is in a judge's hands

Action Steps: Preparing for a Smart Negotiation

1. Know Your Numbers Gather every financial statement, debt, bill, paycheck, and benefit statement you can find. Knowledge is power.
2. Identify Your Needs vs. Wants Prioritize what you actually need to live, work, and care for any children. Differentiate that from what you emotionally want to hold onto.
3. Think Long-Term Run the numbers. If you take the house, can you afford the mortgage, maintenance, insurance, and taxes? If you keep the investments, are you prepared for market ups and downs?
4. Consider Future Income Will you need spousal support? Can you reenter the workforce? Are there opportunities to upskill, go back to school, or start a business?
5. Get Professional Help A divorce financial planner or Certified Divorce Financial Analyst (CDFA) can help you see the full picture.
6. Practice Your Talking Points If you're negotiating directly, rehearse what you need to say. Stay calm, stick to facts, and don't let emotions derail your plan.
7. Don't Rush You might be tempted to "get it over with," but a rushed agreement can cost you years of regret. Take your time. This is your

future.

Negotiating from a Place of Strength

Fair settlements come from clarity. You don't have to be loud or aggressive to stand up for yourself. You need:

- Clear financial records
- A real understanding of what you need to be okay
- A commitment to protecting your future

You are not asking for too much. You are asking for stability. For fairness. For the ability to move forward without falling apart financially. That's not selfish. That's responsible.

Final Thoughts: This Is the Beginning, Not the End

Divorce is the end of a chapter—not your whole story. The decisions you make now will shape the rest of your financial life. So make them from a place of strength, not fear. Of vision, not revenge.

You don't need to win the divorce. You need to win your life back. You need to negotiate a future that supports you, protects you, and lets you walk into the next season with confidence.

So take a deep breath. Gather your numbers. Get good advice.

And know this: fair might not mean equal. But it can absolutely mean empowered.

You deserve that. And more.

Chapter 16: The Emotional Cost of Divorce – And How It Shows Up in Your Finances

Divorce doesn't just crack open the foundation of a marriage; it reverberates through every part of your life—your identity, your routines, your relationships, your energy, and yes, your bank account. You don't just wake up one day with new financial numbers and a signed agreement. You wake up with a different emotional landscape, and it shows up everywhere—especially in your money.

In this chapter, we're going to slow down and talk about the real stuff. Not spreadsheets or credit scores—though those matter too. But about how your emotional world impacts your financial decisions. We'll talk about guilt spending, survival mode, revenge buying, financial anxiety, self-worth, and the deeper layers behind the money moves you're making or avoiding right now.

Because here's the truth: if we don't address what's going on inside, we'll keep repeating the same patterns outside.

Let's get into it.

The Hidden Price of Grief

Even if the divorce was necessary. Even if you were the one who asked for it. Even if it ended amicably. There is grief. There is loss.

You grieve the vision you had of your future. You grieve the routines, the holidays, the shared finances. You grieve the illusion of forever.

And when people grieve, they cope in different ways. Some go numb.

Some stay busy. Some spend.

Grief spending is real. It looks like:

- Impulse shopping to feel better
- Taking a vacation you can't really afford "to reset"
- Signing up for too many streaming subscriptions to fill the silence
- Overbuying for your kids to make up for what they're going through

These are emotional choices disguised as financial ones.

It's not about shame. It's about awareness.

You are allowed to feel all the feelings. But let's work toward not letting the feelings drain your bank account.

Action Step: Pause before every purchase over $100. Ask yourself, "What am I really trying to fix with this swipe?"

Guilt and the Urge to Overcompensate

Maybe you left. Maybe you stayed too long. Maybe you think it's your fault.

However you got here, guilt has a way of showing up in the form of trying to "make it right" with your wallet.

Especially with your kids. You buy more. You say yes more. You soften every "no."

But here's what you need to hear: Kids don't need more stuff. They need stability. They need to see a parent who has a plan. Who is strong enough to say no when it matters.

Overcompensating can bankrupt your healing. It turns money into a stand-in for presence. But presence can't be bought.

Pros of Saying No Sometimes:

- Builds healthy boundaries
- Teaches financial lessons
- Models self-discipline

Cons of Always Saying Yes:

- Increases debt
- Fosters entitlement
- Sacrifices your financial future

Action Step: Set a monthly kid-spending budget. Stick to it. Talk to them about why.

Revenge Spending and Proving a Point

Let's keep it real: sometimes the emotional cost of divorce is tied to proving to your ex—or the world—that you're thriving.

You upgrade your wardrobe. You get a new car. You move into a place that's a stretch, just so no one can say you're "losing."

But revenge spending is a trap. Because the people you're trying to impress or outshine? They're not paying your bills.

And the feeling you're chasing? It doesn't come from stuff. It comes from healing. From peace. From a solid foundation.

Revenge is expensive.

You don't have to prove anything. You don't need permission to start small. You don't need anyone's applause.

You just need your dignity, your vision, and your budget.

Action Step: Every time you want to "show off" a purchase, ask yourself: "Would I still buy this if nobody could see it?"

Anxiety and Decision Fatigue

Your brain is doing a lot right now. You're splitting households. You're trying to survive. You're trying to stay sane.

That alone is enough to drain your decision-making power. Add financial decisions on top of that? It's no wonder you feel overwhelmed.

Financial anxiety can paralyze you or push you into bad decisions. It sounds like:

- "I'll deal with it later."
- "I don't want to look at my accounts."
- "I can't budget because everything is a mess."

But here's what will help you get through the fog:

Action Steps to Reduce Financial Anxiety:

1. Make a list of *every* account (bank, credit card, investment, loan).
2. Write down what you owe or own in each one.
3. Choose one day each week to check your numbers—no more, no less.
4. Celebrate any progress, no matter how small.

Your brain needs structure. So does your money.

Rebuilding Confidence Through Small Wins

After divorce, confidence takes a hit. You question your choices. Your ability to lead. Your value.

That shows up financially as:

- Letting others make decisions for you
- Not negotiating your worth at work
- Staying stuck because "you don't know enough"

You have to build your confidence back like you build a muscle: with reps.

Start Here:

- Learn one financial term a week
- Track your spending for 30 days
- Open a high-yield savings account and fund it with $10

These may seem small. But they build momentum. And momentum builds belief.

You don't need to know everything. You just need to do the next right thing.

The Emotions Behind the Numbers

Behind every financial decision is an emotional one:

- Overspending = I want to feel in control

- Avoiding = I'm afraid of what I'll see
- Giving too much = I want to be loved
- Not saving = I don't think I'm worth it

The numbers are just the result. The root is the belief.

So ask yourself:

- What money story did I grow up with?
- What do I believe money says about me?
- How do I treat myself when I have money?
- How do I treat myself when I don't?

Healing your financial life means telling yourself a new story.

Final Thoughts: Money Is Emotional, and That's Okay

You are not weak for feeling things during this season. You are not behind. You are not broken.

You are navigating one of the hardest transitions of your life, and still showing up to do the work. That is strength.

Keep going. Give yourself grace. Start with one change at a time.

Because the goal isn't just to recover financially. It's to rebuild a life that feels strong, centered, and yours.

Your future self is going to be so proud of how you handled this season.

And your money? It's going to tell the story of your healing.

Part 3: The Rebuild – Starting Fresh Financially

Divorce can feel like a financial earthquake—shaking the foundation of your life and leaving you to pick up the pieces. But in the aftermath comes an opportunity: the chance to rebuild, smarter and stronger. Part 3 is all about that rebuild.

This section walks readers through the essentials of starting over with clarity, control, and confidence. Whether you're managing money solo for the first time in years, rebuilding your credit, or figuring out how to budget on a single income, this part is your guide to regaining your financial footing.

We begin with the basics: how to reassess your financial life post-divorce, create a new budget, and set realistic goals for the short and long term. You'll learn how to evaluate what assets and debts you now hold, rebuild credit with intention, and avoid common pitfalls like lifestyle inflation or emotional overspending.

From there, we move into practical next steps—creating emergency funds, choosing the right accounts, setting up insurance, and beginning to invest again with your future in mind. For many, this is also a time to reevaluate career goals or consider new income streams.

Most importantly, this part helps you shift your mindset. It's not just about recovering—it's about reimagining. Your financial life doesn't have to be a lesser version of what it was. It can be wiser, more empowered, and fully aligned with the person you are becoming.

Because while you may be starting fresh, you are not starting from scratch—you're starting from experience.

Chapter 17: Creating a Post-Divorce Budget That Works

You've been through the fire. The paperwork is signed, the house might feel a little quieter, and now here you are—staring at a bank statement that looks a lot different than it did just a few months ago. You're not alone.

A post-divorce budget isn't just a spreadsheet—it's a lifeline. A map. A way to remind yourself, "Hey, I've got this," even if you're not sure how yet.

Let's build something that works for *you*. Not your ex. Not your financial planner. Not the influencer on Instagram showing off their 'minimalist but luxurious' lifestyle. You.

This chapter is about getting real, getting clear, and getting back in the driver's seat. Together.

First Things First: Breathe

Before we start crunching numbers, I want you to take a deep breath.

Seriously.

The numbers can wait for just one more minute. You've been through one of the most stressful emotional and financial events a person can experience. It makes sense if you're feeling like your entire financial life was just put through a paper shredder.

But this moment—right here, right now—is the starting line of something new.

You're not starting from nothing. You're starting from *experience.* And experience, painful as it might be, is one of the most valuable tools you can have when it comes to building a better financial future.

What a Post-Divorce Budget Really Means

When people hear the word "budget," they often think "restriction" or "sacrifice." That's not what we're doing here.

This isn't about guilt. It's not about shame. It's not about punishing yourself for what happened or what was spent.

This is about *clarity.* It's about designing a plan that supports the life you're rebuilding—a life that fits *your* values, *your* needs, and *your* future.

A good post-divorce budget:

- Helps you understand your new financial reality.
- Gives you control over what you have.
- Helps you plan for what you need.
- Builds toward what you want.

Let's start laying that foundation.

Step 1: Know What You're Working With

Before we can build a plan, we need to know the raw materials.

Income

Start by listing *all* sources of income. Depending on your divorce settlement and current situation, your income might come from:

- Your job (salary, hourly, freelance, or self-employment)
- Alimony or spousal support
- Child support

- Part-time gigs or side hustles
- Investments or passive income
- Pensions or benefits

Action Step:

Write down your monthly *net* income—that's after taxes. If your income is irregular (e.g., freelance), use a 3-6 month average. Be honest. No fluffing it up for how you *hope* it will look. This is your truth, and we can only work with the truth.

Expenses

This part might sting a little. That's okay.

Grab your last two to three months of bank and credit card statements. Go line-by-line. Highlight and sort your spending into categories:

- Housing (rent or mortgage, property taxes, HOA, utilities)
- Food (groceries, dining out, school lunches)
- Transportation (gas, car payment, insurance, Uber)
- Insurance (health, dental, life, home/renters, etc.)
- Child-related expenses (tuition, daycare, clothes, sports, activities)
- Debt payments (credit cards, loans, lines of credit)
- Health (medical co-pays, prescriptions, therapy)
- Subscriptions & memberships
- Entertainment
- Shopping
- Miscellaneous or "surprises"

Action Step:

Tally up your *fixed expenses* (the things you have to pay no matter what) and *variable expenses* (the things you can adjust or eliminate).

This gives you your current financial picture: income vs. expenses.

Chapter 18: Rerouting Retirement – Rebuilding with New Goals

You didn't plan to be here. Not like this.

Maybe you'd envisioned retiring side-by-side with a partner, splitting the cost of a beachfront condo or downsizing together in the suburbs. Maybe you'd imagined grandkids visiting a shared home. Maybe your ex was the one who "handled all the money," and now you're staring at statements, unsure what you're even looking at.

But here you are. Not where you thought you'd be. And that's okay.

Rerouting doesn't mean giving up on the destination. It just means taking a different path to get there.

This chapter is about reclaiming your retirement dream—on your terms. Whether you're 35 or 65, this is your chance to refocus, rebuild, and move forward with clarity. Because retirement is not just about stopping work. It's about security, choice, and peace of mind. And you still deserve all of that.

Let's walk this together.

First, Give Yourself a Moment

Divorce often feels like it unplugs everything—emotionally and financially. And when it comes to retirement, it's common to feel like you've lost time, savings, or stability.

Maybe you had to split a 401(k). Maybe you cashed out a retirement account to afford legal fees. Maybe your ex's pension or Social Security benefits were part of the long-term plan.

Whatever happened, I want you to take a deep breath and know: it's not over. You still have time. You still have options. You still have agency.

This is your *starting point*, not your finish line.

Step One: Inventory What You Have

You can't reroute until you know where you're starting from. We're going to take stock—not in a judgmental way, but in an honest, empowering one.

Create Your Retirement Snapshot

Start by listing every retirement-related asset or potential income stream. That might include:

- 401(k), 403(b), or other workplace retirement accounts
- Traditional IRA or Roth IRA
- SEP IRA or Solo 401(k) if you're self-employed
- Pension (either from your own employment or a portion of your ex's, if awarded in divorce)
- Social Security estimates (yours and possibly your ex's)
- Annuities
- Taxable investment accounts
- Health Savings Account (HSA)
- Cash savings earmarked for retirement

Action Step:

Use a simple notebook or spreadsheet to write down each account's name, balance, owner, and any relevant notes (e.g., "Split with ex during divorce," or "Penalties if withdrawn early").

This is your new foundation. And it's stronger than you think.

Step Two: Understand What Changed

Divorce may have affected your retirement trajectory in subtle or dramatic ways. Here's how to unpack that.

Common Post-Divorce Retirement Shifts

- **You're now saving solo.** No more double-income contribution power.
- **Assets may have been divided.** That nest egg? It might be half the size now.
- **You may have new obligations.** Child support, housing, debt, or legal fees can squeeze your saving capacity.
- **You may need to work longer.** But you also may want to—for personal fulfillment or to regain savings ground.

Emotional Note:

This is where grief often creeps in. You're not just rerouting dollars—you're grieving the version of life that no longer exists. Give yourself space to feel that. Then let's figure out how to move forward.

Step Three: Rework Your Retirement Timeline

Let's get practical.

How Old Are You Now?

Your age impacts how you invest, how much time you have to grow savings, and when you can access certain accounts.

- **Under 50?** You've got time—and you can get aggressive.
- **50–59?** You may qualify for "catch-up contributions." Now's the time to pour it on.

- **60–65?** Time to tighten up your game plan, maximize savings, and reduce risk.
- **Over 65?** Don't panic. You may still be working or eligible for Social Security, Medicare, and creative income strategies.

Action Step:

Write down your current age, your *ideal* retirement age, and your *minimum* retirement income goal (we'll refine this later). This gives us a target to work toward.

Step Four: Set New Retirement Goals

This is one of the most important emotional and financial steps you'll take: *defining what retirement looks like now.*

Questions to Ask Yourself:

- Do I want to fully stop working, or do I want to shift into part-time work, passion projects, or consulting?
- Do I want to stay in my current home or relocate?
- Do I want to travel—or stay rooted near family?
- What does "peaceful" mean to me in retirement?
- What lifestyle feels sustainable and joyful?

There's no right or wrong here. This isn't about what you *should* want—it's about what you *actually* want.

Action Step:

Write a short "retirement vision statement." One paragraph. No numbers—just feelings. This becomes your compass.

Step Five: Calculate Your New Retirement Needs

Let's bring your dream down to earth.

Basic Formula

1. Estimate your desired monthly expenses in retirement.
2. Multiply that by 12 (for annual costs).
3. Multiply that by the number of years you expect to be retired (use 20–30 as a rough range).
4. Subtract any expected income (like Social Security, pension, annuities).
5. The gap? That's what you'll need to save or generate from retirement accounts.

Example:

- Desired monthly retirement income: $4,000
- Annual: $48,000
- 25-year retirement: $1.2 million
- Expected Social Security: $2,000/month ($24,000/year)
- Gap: $24,000/year × 25 years = $600,000

That's your target. But don't let that number scare you. We're about to break it down.

Step Six: Maximize Retirement Savings—Even If You're Starting Late

Divorce might've disrupted your savings. That doesn't mean it's too late.

Strategies by Age & Stage

In Your 30s–40s:

- Max out employer plans (401(k), 403(b))
- Contribute to Roth IRA or Traditional IRA
- Side hustle income? Open a SEP IRA
- Automate your savings monthly

In Your 50s:

- Use catch-up contributions (extra $7,500 in 401(k)s, $1,000 in IRAs)
- Reallocate expenses from kids/house to retirement
- Delay big purchases that could derail compounding
- Consider downsizing to reduce monthly overhead

In Your 60s and Beyond:

- Delay Social Security if possible (benefits increase by ~8% each year you delay past full retirement age)
- Shift investments to a more conservative mix
- Consider part-time income or consulting work
- Minimize taxes by withdrawing from taxable accounts first, then pre-tax

Action Step:

Pick one account—just one—and increase your contribution this month. Even by $25. Progress matters more than perfection.

Step Seven: Consider Working with a Pro (or DIY with Clarity)

You don't have to do this alone.

Pros of Hiring a Financial Advisor

- Helps create a retirement income plan
- Rebalances your investment strategy
- Coordinates tax planning
- Can help you make decisions with less emotion
- May offer hourly or flat-fee plans (if you don't want asset management)

Cons

- May charge high fees if not fee-only
- Not all advisors are fiduciaries (always ask)
- Some prefer to DIY with online tools

Tip:

Ask potential advisors: "Are you a fiduciary?" and "How are you paid?" Clarity matters.

Action Step:

Interview one advisor this month—even just for a consultation. Think of it as research, not commitment.

Step Eight: Don't Forget About Social Security and Divorce Rules

If you were married for **10 years or more**, divorced, and haven't remarried, you may be eligible to receive Social Security based on your *ex's* record.

Key Facts:

- You must be at least 62 to apply.
- Your benefit will be up to 50% of your ex's full retirement benefit.
- Your claim won't reduce your ex's benefits.
- You must not be remarried (unless your later marriage also ended).
- If you qualify for your own benefit and your ex's, you'll receive the higher of the two (not both).

Action Step:

Visit ssa.gov and use the retirement estimator. You may also need to call to discuss divorce-related eligibility.

Step Nine: Make a Retirement Budget—Yes, Even Now

Retirement isn't just about saving—it's about spending *wisely* later.

Start imagining what your retirement budget might look like.

Categories to Include:

- Housing (rent, mortgage, taxes)
- Utilities
- Groceries
- Healthcare premiums + out-of-pocket
- Travel
- Insurance (Medicare Supplement, Long-Term Care, etc.)
- Entertainment
- Family support (gifts, help for adult children)
- Inflation cushion

Tip:

Build in a "fun fund." Retirement should be lived, not just survived.

Step Ten: Keep Going—Even if the Path Changes Again

Life will keep shifting. That's okay.

Maybe you'll remarry. Maybe you'll want to retire earlier than planned. Maybe you'll switch careers, move states, or help a child through college.

The plan doesn't need to be rigid—it just needs to be *responsive.*

You've already proven you can pivot. Now you're pivoting with purpose.

Reflection: You've Come So Far

This isn't just about money. It's about reclaiming your voice in your financial future.

You're building something. You're saying, "I still get to dream. I still get to plan. I still get to have peace."

Keep walking forward. Keep asking questions. Keep adjusting your sails.

Your retirement may look different than you once pictured—but it can still be beautiful.

Step Eleven: Downsizing—More Than Just a Smaller House

One of the most powerful financial levers you have in this season is your lifestyle.

When we talk about "downsizing," we're not just talking about square footage. We're talking about *right-sizing* your life to match your new goals, your new budget, and your new peace.

What Downsizing Could Look Like:

- Selling a large family home for something smaller and easier to maintain
- Moving closer to adult children or grandkids to reduce travel expenses
- Relocating to a more tax-friendly state
- Letting go of second homes or rental properties that cause more stress than income

- Releasing material possessions tied to your old life that no longer serve your vision for retirement

Emotional Reality Check:

It's okay to grieve what you're leaving behind. That house held memories. Those things had meaning. But what you're moving toward now is *freedom*. Lower bills. Less upkeep. A simpler life that supports your emotional and financial health.

Pros of Downsizing:

- Cuts mortgage or rent expenses
- Reduces utility and maintenance costs
- May provide a cash boost from equity
- Simplifies day-to-day life
- Encourages a fresh start

Cons (and How to Navigate Them):

- Emotional attachment to your current home
- *Strategy:* Focus on what you're gaining: peace, freedom, lower bills, and room for the next chapter.
- Moving can be stressful
- *Strategy:* Take it slow. Ask for help. Hire movers. Give yourself grace.
- Friends or support systems might be farther away
- *Strategy:* Stay connected. Build new community through volunteering, faith groups, or local activities.

Action Step:

Run the numbers. What would it save you monthly—and annually—to downsize? Where could that money go instead (investments, travel, savings, fun)?

Step Twelve: Get Creative About Generating Income in Retirement

You may be "retired," but that doesn't mean you can't *earn*. In fact, many divorcees find a surprising amount of fulfillment (and financial stability) from creative income streams in retirement.

Ideas for Income in Retirement:

1. Part-Time Work You Enjoy

- Consulting in your old profession
- Teaching (online or locally)
- Freelance or contract work
- Retail or service jobs with social interaction

2. Turn a Passion Into a Side Hustle

- Writing, photography, crafting, or art
- Coaching, mentoring, or public speaking
- Selling on Etsy, eBay, or Facebook Marketplace
- Airbnb a spare room or vacation rental

3. Monetize Skills You Already Have

- Bookkeeping
- Resume writing or editing
- Childcare or tutoring
- Pet-sitting or dog walking

4. Real Estate Income

- Rent out a basement or garage apartment

- Purchase a small rental property (carefully)
- House hack: live in one side of a duplex, rent the other

Why This Works

- Adds cushion to your retirement budget
- Keeps you mentally and socially active
- Allows you to delay drawing from retirement accounts
- Can help you stay below certain tax brackets or Medicare thresholds

Pros:

- Financial flexibility
- Personal fulfillment
- Can reduce boredom or isolation

Cons:

- Time commitment
- Risk of burnout
- May affect Social Security taxes if under full retirement age

Action Step:

Make a list of five things you're good at or enjoy. Then brainstorm one way each of those things could be turned into an income stream. Keep it fun. Keep it doable.

Step Thirteen: Rebalance Your Portfolio for Your New Reality

Investing after divorce is different. You're working with a new set of assets, new timeframes, and new risks.

Let's break down what matters most now.

Key Retirement Investing Concepts (Plain English Style):

Asset Allocation:

This is how your money is divided between stocks (risky but grow), bonds (safer but slower), and cash (safe but earns little).

Risk Tolerance:

How comfortable are you with ups and downs in the market? The closer you are to retirement, the more you want to reduce big swings.

Rebalancing:

Over time, your portfolio shifts on its own. Rebalancing means adjusting it back to your target—so you don't end up too risky (or too conservative).

Example:

Let's say your ideal allocation is:

- 60% stocks
- 30% bonds
- 10% cash

After a strong stock market year, your portfolio might shift to 70/20/10. That's riskier than you intended. Rebalancing means selling some stocks and buying bonds to get back to 60/30/10.

Tools to Help:

- Robo-advisors (like Betterment, Wealthfront)
- Target-date retirement funds (adjust automatically over time)
- Financial advisors or retirement planners

Action Step:

Check your current allocation. Is it aligned with your new risk tolerance and timeline? If not, it's time to rebalance.

Step Fourteen: Be Strategic About Taxes

Divorce changes your tax picture. And retirement adds a whole new layer. Here's what you need to know—without the headache.

Understand Account Types

1. **Pre-tax Accounts (401(k), Traditional IRA)**
   You pay taxes *when* you withdraw the money.
2. **After-tax Accounts (Roth IRA)**
   You paid taxes upfront—so withdrawals are tax-free in retirement.
3. **Taxable Investment Accounts**
   You pay capital gains tax on profits when you sell investments.

Smart Strategies Post-Divorce:

- Consider a Roth conversion (move money from Traditional IRA to Roth IRA)—especially in years with lower income.
- Use a Health Savings Account (HSA) to pay for qualified medical expenses tax-free.
- Spread out withdrawals from different account types to manage your tax bracket.

Social Security Tax Traps:

- If your combined income (includes half of your Social Security + other income) exceeds $25,000 (single), up to 85% of your benefits can be taxed.

Action Step:

Talk to a CPA or tax planner familiar with retirement. A 30-minute session could save you thousands.

Step Fifteen: Watch Out for Common Retirement Traps

Don't let fear or pressure drive your decisions now. Awareness is protection.

Trap 1: Overhelping Adult Children

Yes, you love them. Yes, you want to support them. But if you drain your retirement to help them now, they may end up supporting you later.

Solution:

Set boundaries. Help in non-financial ways. Offer emotional, not just financial, support.

Trap 2: Taking Social Security Too Early

You can claim as early as 62, but you'll get *less* than if you wait until full retirement age (66–67). Waiting until 70? You'll receive about 132% of your full benefit.

Solution:

If you can afford to wait, it pays to delay.

Trap 3: Going Too Conservative Too Soon

Retirement can last 25+ years. If you move everything into cash, inflation will eat away your buying power.

Solution:

Keep some growth-oriented investments, even in retirement. Think: 40–60% stocks, depending on age and goals.

Trap 4: Thinking It's Too Late

It's not. I don't care if you're 60, 65, or 70. If you're breathing, you still have time to make smart moves.

Solution:

Start where you are. Small steps. Consistent action.

Step Sixteen: Redefine What "Success" Looks Like

You might not retire on a yacht. You might not have matching His-and-Hers Adirondack chairs overlooking the ocean.

But you might travel twice a year with your sister.

You might volunteer with kids and wake up every day with purpose.

You might finally start the garden you've always dreamed of.

You might live a smaller life with a bigger smile.

Success isn't what it *used* to look like. And that's okay.

This version of retirement—yours—is full of possibility. Let it be yours, fully and freely.

Chapter 19: Housing Decisions – Renting, Buying, Downsizing, or Starting Over

Let's be honest—when your whole life shifts, your living situation often comes right along with it.

Maybe you're still in the same house, but it suddenly feels empty. Maybe you had to move quickly and are now figuring out what comes next. Maybe you're asking yourself: *Can I afford to stay here? Do I even want to?*

Housing is more than just bricks and square footage. It's safety. It's memory. It's identity. And after divorce, it can also be one of the biggest emotional and financial decisions you'll make.

This chapter is about helping you make that decision from a place of power—not panic.

So let's walk through the real questions, real options, and real strategies to help you find not just a place to live, but a place to rebuild.

Start Here: You Don't Owe Anyone a "Forever" Decision

One of the first things I want to tell you is this: **You don't have to figure it all out right away.**

Housing decisions after divorce can feel massive. You're juggling emotions, finances, logistics, and possibly children, all at once. Give yourself permission to pause, breathe, and make the next *right* step—not necessarily the perfect one.

This chapter isn't here to tell you what to do. It's here to walk you through the options, help you understand the trade-offs, and build your confidence to choose what's best for *you* in this season.

The Big Question: Should You Stay or Should You Go?

One of the first forks in the road after divorce is this: Do I stay in the home I shared with my ex—or do I go?

It's not just a financial question. It's emotional. And layered.

Let's break it down.

Reasons You Might Want to Stay:

- Familiarity for kids and routines
- Emotional attachment to the space
- Good mortgage terms or equity
- Close to school, work, or family

Reasons You Might Consider Leaving:

- The mortgage or maintenance is no longer affordable
- Too many painful memories
- Too much space (or not enough)
- A fresh start feels necessary

Action Step:

Make two lists—"Reasons to Stay" and "Reasons to Leave." Be brutally honest with yourself. Don't just look at the numbers. Look at how each option makes you feel, too.

Option 1: Staying in the Marital Home

If you're considering staying, you need to get real about whether it's emotionally and financially sustainable.

Key Questions:

- Is the home in your name, your ex's name, or both?
- Did the divorce decree include who keeps the house?
- Can you afford the mortgage and upkeep on your income alone?
- Will refinancing be required to remove your ex's name or buy out their share?

Pros of Staying:

- Stability (especially for children)
- No immediate moving costs
- Emotional grounding during transition

Cons of Staying:

- Can be financially draining on a single income
- You're responsible for all maintenance, taxes, and repairs
- Could prevent you from downsizing and investing the equity elsewhere

Tip:

If the home is paid off or has a low mortgage, staying might make sense. But if it stretches you thin each month, it could become an anchor instead of a refuge.

Action Step:

Get a full picture of your monthly housing costs: mortgage, taxes, insurance, HOA, utilities, maintenance. Compare it against your current post-divorce income. Is it sustainable for the next 5+ years?

Option 2: Selling the House and Starting Fresh

If staying isn't feasible—or simply isn't healthy—selling the house may be your best option. And that's okay.

Selling is not failure. It's transition.

Pros of Selling:

- Access to home equity (if any) for your next chapter
- Lower monthly expenses in a smaller place
- Emotional closure and a fresh start
- Opportunity to relocate if needed

Cons of Selling:

- Emotional grief or sense of loss
- Moving logistics and costs
- Navigating the real estate market post-divorce

Emotional Insight:

Don't underestimate the power of a fresh space. One that's all yours. No shared memories. Just new energy.

Action Step:

Contact a real estate agent you trust and ask for a comparative market analysis (CMA) to get a sense of what your home is worth today. Ask them to estimate net proceeds after mortgage payoff and fees.

Option 3: Renting—The Pause Button with Power

Renting doesn't mean giving up. It means giving yourself breathing room.

In fact, for many recently divorced folks, renting is the smartest short-term move.

Pros of Renting:

- Flexibility—no long-term commitment
- Fewer responsibilities (no maintenance, property taxes, repairs)
- Allows time to rebuild credit or save for a new down payment
- Opportunity to try a new neighborhood or city before committing

Cons of Renting:

- Rent can increase over time
- No equity-building
- May feel temporary or less "settled"

When Renting Makes Sense:

- You're unsure where you want to live long-term
- You're recovering financially and need lower monthly costs
- You're emotionally exhausted and need simplicity

Action Step:

Explore rental options in neighborhoods you'd feel safe and supported in. Look at your budget and determine how much you can afford to spend in rent while still saving for future goals.

Option 4: Buying Again—On Your Own Terms

Eventually, you might be ready to buy again. And this time, you get to make all the decisions.

No compromises on location. No arguments about countertops. Just you—and your priorities.

Key Considerations Before Buying:

- Do you have a stable source of income?
- Do you have 3–6 months of emergency savings?
- Is your credit score healthy enough to qualify for a good loan?
- Can you afford the down payment, closing costs, and ongoing maintenance?

Pros of Buying:

- Stability and control
- Equity-building over time
- Opportunity to personalize and make it your own

Cons of Buying:

- Less flexibility than renting
- Upfront costs (down payment, inspection, closing)
- Ongoing responsibility for repairs and taxes

Action Step:

Use an online mortgage calculator to run scenarios for different home prices. Don't just ask, "How much house can I afford?" Ask, "How much can I afford *comfortably* while still saving and living?"

The Role of Emotion in Housing Decisions

Let's talk about the elephant in the room: how it *feels* to make housing choices post-divorce.

Your home may have been your anchor. Or it may have been a battleground. Either way, housing is emotionally loaded.

Give yourself grace for whatever comes up:

- Grief over letting go of a dream
- Guilt about uprooting kids
- Anxiety about finances
- Hope for something new

There is no "right" way to feel. There is only *your* way.

And your feelings? They matter. Let them speak—but don't let them make decisions alone. Invite your head and your heart to the table.

Housing and Kids: What to Consider

If you're a parent, your housing decisions don't just impact you. They ripple out to your children's sense of safety, stability, and belonging.

Things to Think About:

- School districts and commute times
- Proximity to co-parent (if shared custody)
- Bedroom setups—do the kids have their own space?
- Will moving affect their social or emotional wellbeing?

Note:

You don't have to give your kids everything they had before. You just have to give them love, consistency, and your presence.

It's okay if the house is smaller. It's okay if you rent for a while. What they need most is *you*—whole and healing.

Credit, Mortgages, and Starting Over Financially

Let's get into some real talk about the practical side of things.

Divorce can leave credit bruised. Joint accounts, missed payments, legal fees—it adds up.

But you can recover.

Steps to Rebuild Credit:

1. **Check your credit reports** from all three bureaus (Experian, TransUnion, Equifax) at annualcreditreport.com.
2. **Dispute inaccuracies**, especially if old joint accounts were paid off or closed.
3. **Open a secured credit card** if needed to rebuild slowly.
4. **Pay every bill on time.** Automate it if you have to.
5. **Keep balances low**—aim for under 30% of your credit limit.

Once your credit begins to rebound, your options for mortgages and homeownership open back up.

When You Need to Move Quickly

Sometimes, the decision isn't really a decision at all. The house was sold in the divorce. The rent is up. You've got 30 days.

In those cases, focus on:

- Affordability first
- Safety and location second
- Long-term preferences later

This might be a temporary stop on your way to something better. That's okay. You're not settling—you're *stabilizing*.

Action Step:

Make a list of must-haves and nice-to-haves for a short-term rental. Lean into practicality. Look for places with flexible lease terms, utilities included, or move-in specials.

Reflection: Home Is What You Make It

No matter where you end up—in a condo, an apartment, a house, or a small guest room while you regroup—remember this:

Home is not the square footage. It's how you feel inside it.

You get to decide what peace looks like now. What comfort looks like. What stability means for you.

Whether you're renting or buying, downsizing or upsizing, moving away or staying put—you're not running from the past. You're building something new. Something that fits who you are now.

Chapter 20: Opening New Accounts – Banking, Credit Cards, and Setting Boundaries

You're Not Starting Over—You're Starting Fresh

There's a difference between starting over and starting fresh. Starting over sounds like you've lost something. Like you're back at square one, stripped of your resources, your confidence, your rhythm. But starting fresh? That's about clarity. Intention. Power. It's about saying, "This time, I get to choose."

And that's where you are now—with the chance to choose your financial path.

In this chapter, we're going to walk through how to open new financial accounts—bank accounts, credit cards, and accounts that help rebuild your independence and security. We'll also talk about boundaries—because emotional boundaries and financial boundaries are often connected, especially after divorce. You'll learn what's essential, what's optional, what to watch out for, and how to move forward one account—and one confident choice—at a time.

Let's take a breath. You've already made it through the hardest part. Now it's time to rebuild on *your* terms.

Why New Accounts Matter After Divorce

Divorce doesn't just split homes and households—it splits money. Joint accounts, shared credit cards, co-signed loans, all the things you once built together now require separation. Emotionally, that's heavy. But logistically, it's also necessary.

Here's why it matters:

- **You need financial autonomy.** Your money, your choices.
- **You need a clean break.** No lingering joint ties that can come back to bite you.
- **You need clarity.** So you can track your income, bills, and progress without confusion.

Even if the separation was amicable, even if you still get along, shared financial accounts can muddy the waters. One person overdrafts the joint account—your credit gets dinged. One person misses a credit card payment—you both suffer.

So, yes, it's time to open new accounts. Not out of spite, but out of self-respect. Let's dive in.

Step One: Opening a New Bank Account

What You Need:

- Your Social Security number
- Government-issued ID (driver's license, passport)
- Proof of address (utility bill, lease, etc.)
- Initial deposit (this can be as little as $25–$100)

Checking vs. Savings

- **Checking account** – This is your money-in, money-out account. Think of it like your financial home base. Your paycheck lands here. Your bills get paid from here.
- **Savings account** – This is where your short-term and emergency money should live. Ideally, it earns a little interest and stays untouched unless absolutely needed.

Pros of Starting Fresh:

- Clean separation from joint accounts
- Easier budgeting and tracking
- Full control over your cash flow
- Stronger financial identity post-divorce

Cons:

- If you're used to joint income, it may feel like less at first
- Adjusting to managing solo can be stressful at the start
- May require updating direct deposits and bill pay

Action Steps:

1. Choose a bank that aligns with your values—big bank, credit union, or online bank?
2. Go online or visit a branch and open your new checking and savings accounts.
3. Set up direct deposit for your income (job, alimony, child support, etc.).
4. Update automatic payments to come from your new account.
5. Close or remove yourself from all joint accounts.

Step Two: Rebuilding (or Reclaiming) Your Credit

Let's be real—divorce can mess with your credit.

Maybe your name was on the mortgage and the bills weren't paid. Maybe you co-signed on a credit card that's now maxed out. Maybe you're starting with no credit history at all.

Whatever the case, it's okay. You're not alone, and you're not stuck.

Why Credit Matters:

- It impacts your ability to rent a place, get a car, or refinance anything
- It can affect job applications in some industries
- It determines the interest rates you'll be offered on loans or credit cards

How to Rebuild It:

- **Get a secured credit card.** These are backed by a deposit you make (say, $300). Use it like a regular card, pay it off in full every month, and your credit grows.
- **Become an authorized user.** If a trusted friend or family member adds you to their card with a good history, it can boost your score.
- **Pay all bills on time.** This is the single most important factor in your credit score.
- **Check your credit report.** Go to www.annualcreditreport.com and review for errors or old joint debts that need to be closed.

Action Steps:

1. Apply for a secured card or starter card with a low limit.
2. Use it for small, regular expenses (like gas or groceries).
3. Pay it off every month—*no exceptions.*
4. Keep credit usage under 30% of your limit.
5. Dispute any errors on your credit report.

Step Three: Setting Boundaries – Financial and Emotional

This part may be harder than opening a bank account. But it's just as important.

After divorce, boundaries are everything. Emotional ones. Financial ones. Communication ones. And if you share kids or mutual friends, those boundaries become even more essential.

What Are Financial Boundaries?

- No more joint spending or accounts.
- Clear agreements on child support or alimony.
- Deciding what you will and won't pay for moving forward.
- Saying *no* when someone expects you to cover costs out of guilt.

Emotional Spending Is Real

We need to talk about emotional spending. It's easy to soothe a broken heart with a shopping spree. A new couch. That $300 pair of boots. But healing isn't for sale. You won't find peace at checkout.

Before every purchase, ask yourself:

- Is this a *need* or a *numbing*?
- Am I spending to impress, distract, or escape?
- Will this purchase make me feel better long-term?

Action Steps:

1. Write a post-divorce budget. Include every expense you control.
2. Set spending limits for discretionary items (clothes, entertainment, etc.).
3. Identify spending triggers—what leads to impulse buys?
4. Practice saying "no" without apology—to others and to yourself.

5. Create a "cooling-off" rule: wait 24 hours before large purchases.

Choosing the Right Tools and Technology

Let's make life easier. You've got enough on your plate. There are tools that can help you stay on top of your finances with less effort.

Useful Apps and Platforms:

- **Mint or YNAB (You Need a Budget)** – Budget tracking and planning.
- **Credit Karma** – Free credit monitoring and score updates.
- **Bank apps** – For mobile deposits, transfers, and spending alerts.
- **Truebill/Rocket Money** – Helps cancel unwanted subscriptions and renegotiate bills.

Action Steps:

1. Download a budget app and start tracking every dollar.
2. Set up automatic savings—even if it's just $10 a week.
3. Use spending alerts to avoid overdraft or impulse purchases.
4. Monitor your credit regularly and watch your progress.

(continued in next message...)

(continued from previous message...)

Knowing What to Avoid

In the emotional fog of divorce, it's easy to make rushed financial choices. Some of these decisions can have long-lasting consequences. So let's slow it down and take a clear-eyed look at what to steer clear of.

Watch Out For:

- **Store credit cards** – High interest, low limits, and often predatory.
- **Co-signing for anyone** – Especially an ex or new partner. Don't do it.
- **Joint loans or credit cards post-divorce** – It may feel familiar, but it's risky.
- **Financial predators** – Anyone who promises "quick credit fixes" or miracle solutions to debt.
- **New romantic partners pressuring you financially** – Red flag. Full stop.

Action Steps:

1. Say no to all joint accounts going forward—yes, even small ones.
2. Avoid borrowing from retirement to "catch up" unless guided by a professional.
3. Don't fall for financial scams. If it sounds too good to be true, it is.
4. Trust your gut. If something feels off—pause and ask for advice.

Creating a New Money Identity

Divorce forces you to redefine so much—your home, your name, your routines. But it also gives you the opportunity to redefine how you show up financially. This is your chance to write a new money story. One that reflects who you are now—and who you want to become.

Ask Yourself:

- What did I learn about money in my marriage?
- What money habits do I want to leave behind?
- What would financial peace feel like to me?
- What do I want my kids (if any) to learn from watching me now?

A New Financial Identity Might Include:

- **Confidence in making financial decisions.**
- **A calm, organized relationship with money.**
- **A solid credit score.**
- **Savings that grow.**
- **The ability to say no—and mean it.**

This isn't just about accounts and numbers. This is about walking into your bank or logging into your account and *feeling good.* Like you belong there. Like you're in charge. Because you are.

Case Studies: Real Stories, Real Recovery

Rachel, 42

After 15 years of marriage, Rachel had never handled the money. Her ex managed everything. Post-divorce, she was terrified. But she opened a new account at a local credit union, started tracking every expense, and used a secured credit card to rebuild her score from 540 to 695 in 18 months. She now teaches her two daughters about budgeting and earns extra income as a freelance writer.

Malik, 50

Malik's divorce left him with joint credit card debt and a feeling of failure. He wanted to provide for his kids but struggled to keep up with child support and bills. By consolidating his accounts, renegotiating payment plans, and meeting with a nonprofit credit counselor, he slowly rebuilt. He now has his own account, a savings cushion, and the peace of knowing he's doing the best he can.

You don't need a financial degree to rebuild—you need a plan, consistency, and grace.

Reflect, Don't Regret

Let's stop here for a moment. Take a breath.

You are not behind.

You are not broken.

You are not irresponsible.

You are learning—because life handed you a situation that requires learning.

Every person who's ever rebuilt financially after a divorce had to start somewhere. And this? This is your start. With clarity. With intention. With a little more wisdom than before.

So whether you're opening a new checking account this week or you're still staring at your old online banking logins trying to let go—know this: You are doing the work. That matters.

Encouragement Before You Go

You may feel overwhelmed right now. That's normal.

You may feel shame for not having "figured it out sooner." That's not your burden to carry.

You may be scared to take that first step alone. That's okay, too.

But I promise you this—there's power in your pause. There's strength in your willingness to rebuild, even when your heart is heavy. There's hope in every password reset, every new debit card, every dollar you set aside for the future you're creating.

You're not just opening new accounts. You're opening up space—for independence. For healing. For peace.

This chapter isn't the end. It's the start of your next strong season.

Expanded Section: Real Stories, Real Recovery (continued)

Lisa, 38 – "I Never Thought I'd Be the One Handling It All"

Lisa spent her entire marriage as a stay-at-home mom. When the divorce papers came, she felt financially paralyzed. She hadn't had a bank account in her own name since college. But with the support of a women's resource center and a therapist, she slowly stepped into her power.

She opened a checking account at a credit union, started tracking every grocery receipt, and signed up for a class on credit basics. When she applied for a secured card, she used it only for gas, paid it off each week, and slowly watched her confidence rise alongside her score. Two years later, Lisa has her own emergency fund, part-time income, and says, "I feel more independent than I ever did married."

Expanded Tools + Tech Guide: What's in Your Digital Wallet?

Technology is your friend in this process. You don't need to do this with spreadsheets and sticky notes (unless that works for you!). Here's a deeper dive into the tools that can support your next chapter.

Budgeting & Tracking:

- **You Need A Budget (YNAB)**: This app helps you give every dollar a job and teaches you how to plan ahead.
- **EveryDollar**: Great for beginners who want a simple, clean layout.
- **Goodbudget**: Envelope-style budgeting that helps you track cash flow in real time.

Credit Tracking:

- **Experian Boost**: Lets you add utility and streaming service payments to help improve your score.
- **MyFICO**: The most accurate source for checking your true FICO score (usually paid).

Bill Management:

- **Prism**: Combines all your bills in one place with reminders.
- **Rocket Money**: Helps you cancel subscriptions, negotiate bills, and see where your money is going.

Emotional Support + Habits:

- **Tiller**: For spreadsheet lovers who want automation.
- **Cleo**: A quirky AI chatbot that gives you tough love on spending and savings goals.

Setting Boundaries: Real Scenarios and Scripts

Setting boundaries can be awkward at first—especially if you're used to people-pleasing, conflict-avoidance, or financial codependence. Here are practical situations you might face and how to navigate them:

1. Your Ex Asks to "Just Use Your Card" Until Payday

> Boundary: *"I'm not comfortable sharing accounts anymore. I need to keep things separate so I can rebuild and stay on track."*

2. A New Partner Pressures You to Go In on a Big Purchase

> Boundary: *"I'm working on building financial stability on my own right now. I'd rather wait until we have a stronger foundation before sharing money decisions."*

3. A Friend Keeps Asking to Borrow Money

> Boundary: *"I care about you, but I've made a commitment to myself not to lend money while I'm rebuilding. I hope you understand."*

4. Your Teenager Doesn't Understand the New Budget

> Boundary: *"Things are different now, and I need to be more careful with how we spend. I'll always make sure you have what you need, and I'll be honest with you along the way."*

Boundaries are not walls—they're gates. They don't lock people out. They protect what you're building. They say, "This is my new beginning, and I'm going to guard it with care."

Financial Red Flags in New Relationships

It's tempting to jump into something new—especially when you're lonely, craving connection, or finally feeling desired again. But beware of love bombing with a price tag.

Red Flags to Watch Out For:

- They ask you to co-sign anything early on.
- They need to "borrow" money repeatedly.
- They discourage you from having your own accounts.
- They guilt you into financial decisions with emotional manipulation.
- They get angry or defensive when you talk about money.

Financial abuse can wear many masks. Just because someone's charming doesn't mean they're trustworthy. Take your time. Protect your peace.

Guided Budget Walkthrough: Your First Post-Divorce Budget

You don't need fancy formulas. You need clarity and control. Let's walk through how to build a budget you can actually stick to.

Step 1: Know Your Income

- Job income
- Child support
- Alimony
- Government benefits
- Side hustles

Step 2: List Your Fixed Expenses

- Rent/mortgage
- Car payment
- Insurance
- Utilities
- Cell phone
- Subscriptions

Step 3: Track Variable Expenses

- Groceries
- Gas
- Eating out
- Kids' activities
- Personal care

Step 4: Add in Savings Goals

- Emergency fund
- Retirement contributions
- Sinking funds (holiday, car repair, etc.)

Step 5: Reality Check

- Are you overspending?
- Where can you trim?
- What can be delayed?

Step 6: Set a Weekly Check-In

- Review your bank app
- Update your tracking system
- Reflect on what worked and what didn't

Reflection Prompts: Journal Your Growth

Before we close, take a few minutes to reflect on your journey so far. Grab a journal or your Notes app and write your honest thoughts.

1. What has been the hardest part of reclaiming your financial independence?
2. What surprised you the most about managing money on your own?
3. What are you proud of?
4. What habits do you want to leave behind?
5. What's one financial goal you want to hit in the next six months?

Write without judgment. This isn't about perfection. It's about progress.

Encouragement: You're Worth the Effort

You may not see the results yet. But they're coming.

Every dollar saved. Every bill paid. Every time you say "no" to protect your peace. That's progress. That's healing. That's power.

You are not behind. You are building. You are not broken. You are becoming.

Keep showing up for yourself. Keep protecting your peace. Keep choosing clarity over chaos, dignity over drama, and purpose over pressure.

Opening new accounts is just the start. The real journey? Reclaiming your life. And you're doing it.

Chapter 21: Protecting Yourself Going Forward – Insurance and Legal Documents

This Time, You're Not Just Surviving—You're Securing

Let's pause for a second and take a breath. You've been through the emotional storm. You've cried in court bathrooms. You've sat on the floor with bills you didn't know how to sort. You've made it through the maze of separation. Now, you're building. Not just rebuilding—you're *securing*. Securing your future, your peace of mind, your right to rest easy at night.

And that starts with protection.

Not just emotional protection, though that matters deeply. We're talking about real-world, nuts-and-bolts protection: the kind that shows up in your mailbox with policy numbers and notarized seals. Insurance. Legal documents. Boring on the surface, but powerful in practice.

This chapter will walk you through exactly what you need to protect yourself now that you're on your own—because you're not just planning for today. You're planning for everything life could throw at you from here on out.

Why Protection Matters More After Divorce

You're no longer part of a financial team. That doesn't mean you're vulnerable—it means you need different gear for the game.

Before, you may have shared benefits, joint life insurance, a will written with "we" instead of "me." Now? You need solo tools for a solo path.

Here's why insurance and legal docs matter:

- They protect your income, your family, and your future from unexpected loss or legal chaos.
- They establish your wishes clearly, so others don't decide for you.
- They create peace of mind that no one—not your ex, not the courts, not chance—will dictate your future without your input.

It's about control. Choice. Dignity.

Section 1: Health Insurance – Don't Let Gaps Leave You Exposed

The Divorce Health Insurance Shock

Many people—especially those who stayed home, worked part-time, or earned less—lose health insurance after divorce. If you were on your ex's employer plan, that coverage usually ends with the divorce decree. That's a scary moment.

Your Options:

1. **COBRA Coverage** – You stay on your ex's plan for up to 36 months, but you pay the full cost (often 2–3x what you paid before).

- *Pros*: Familiar doctors, same coverage.
- *Cons*: Very expensive. Not a long-term fix.

1. **Marketplace/ACA Plans** – Through healthcare.gov or your state exchange.

- *Pros*: Tax credits may make this affordable or even free. Variety of coverage levels.
- *Cons*: Learning curve. May require new providers.

1. **Employer Coverage** – If you have a job with benefits.

- *Pros*: Often the cheapest and most comprehensive.
- *Cons*: Not always an option if you're unemployed or part-time.

1. **Medicaid** – For lower-income individuals.

- *Pros*: Comprehensive and free or low-cost.
- *Cons*: Eligibility varies by state. Not available to all.

Action Steps:

- Find out when your current coverage ends (often the last day of the month your divorce is finalized).
- Use that deadline to apply for COBRA or ACA within 60 days (it's a qualifying life event).
- Compare costs and coverage carefully—don't just go with the first option.

Section 2: Life Insurance – Cover What Matters Now

Life After Joint Policies

If you and your ex had a joint policy or named each other as beneficiaries, it's time to reevaluate.

If you have children, life insurance is not optional—it's essential. Even if you're young, even if you're healthy, even if you feel like you don't have "assets." Your income, your parenting role, your caregiving—all of it needs protection.

Types of Life Insurance:

- **Term Life** – Coverage for a set period (10–30 years). Affordable and simple.
- **Whole Life** – Lasts your entire life and builds cash value. More expensive.
- **Group Life** – Offered by employers. May be limited and not portable if you change jobs.

What to Do Now:

- Check who's listed as your beneficiary. If it's your ex, do you want that to stay the same?
- If you rely on your ex for child support or alimony, you may want *them* to carry life insurance naming *you* or your child as beneficiary.
- Consider buying your own term policy that covers your income until your kids are grown or your debts are paid.

Pros:

- Protects your children or loved ones financially.
- Inexpensive if purchased young and healthy.
- Gives peace of mind.

Cons:

- Premiums can be high if you wait too long or have health issues.
- Must stay organized about renewal periods and beneficiary updates.

Section 3: Disability Insurance – Your Income Is Your Biggest Asset

You might think your house is your biggest asset—but it's not. Your ability to earn money is. If illness or injury takes that away, everything can fall apart quickly.

Divorced or not, if you work and rely on your income, you need disability coverage.

Short-Term vs. Long-Term:

- **Short-Term Disability**: Pays a percentage of your income for a few weeks or months.
- **Long-Term Disability**: Kicks in after short-term ends and can cover you until retirement age.

Check to see if your employer offers group disability coverage. If not, individual policies are available.

Action Steps:

- Ask your HR department if you're covered.
- If not, get quotes from private insurance companies.
- Prioritize long-term over short-term if budget is limited.
- Section 4: Auto and Homeowners/Renters Insurance – Update and Untangle
- Rethinking Insurance After the Split

Did you share a car or a home? Were you bundled on insurance? Did your ex manage the policies? Then it's time to untangle.

If you've moved to a new place, downsized, or bought a car in your own name, your insurance needs have changed. This isn't just a box to check—it's a chance to align your coverage with your new life.

- What to Review:
- **Auto Insurance**: Remove your ex from the policy if you shared one. Make sure your car is titled in your name alone before making changes.
- **Homeowners Insurance**: If you kept the house, update the policy to reflect sole ownership.
- **Renters Insurance**: If you moved into an apartment or rental, this is your safety net. It protects everything you own from theft, fire, and damage.
- Pros:
- Keeps you covered in case of accidents or unexpected events.
- Proof of independence—your name, your asset, your policy.
- Allows for more accurate budgeting based on your new lifestyle.
- Cons:
- May increase premiums if you lost a multi-policy discount.
- Can be confusing if your ex handled this before.
- Action Steps:
- Call your current providers and request updated quotes in your name alone.
- Compare policies from multiple companies—don't just stick with what you had.
- Cancel all shared policies after your new ones are active.
- Section 5: Legal Documents – Rewriting the Fine Print of Your Life
- What Needs to Change

Let's get into the meat of what most people avoid after divorce—*the legal stuff*. But here's the truth: if you don't update your legal documents, someone else could make choices you never agreed to.

Think of legal docs as the GPS for your money, your health, and your legacy. If you're not driving, someone else will—and they may take you down a road you never wanted to go.

- Documents to Revisit:
- **Will**

- If your ex is named as executor or beneficiary, that may no longer reflect your wishes.
- If you don't have a will, state law will decide what happens to your assets.
- **Healthcare Power of Attorney**
- This document lets someone make medical decisions for you if you're incapacitated.
- Do you still want your ex making those decisions?
- **Financial Power of Attorney**
- Gives someone legal access to manage your finances if you can't.
- Choose someone trustworthy and organized—not necessarily a family member.
- **Living Will (Advance Directive)**
- States your preferences about life support, resuscitation, and other care.
- Crucial to have in place to avoid family disputes.
- **Guardianship for Children**
- If you're the primary parent, your will should state who you want to care for your kids if something happens to you.
- **Trusts (Optional but Worth Considering)**
- Especially useful if you have minor children or want to control how assets are used after your death.
- Legal Terms in Plain English

Let's slow down and translate some legalese.

- **Executor**: The person who carries out your will.
- **Beneficiary**: The person who receives money or assets.
- **Power of Attorney (POA)**: Someone you name to make decisions for you if you can't.
- **Guardian**: The person who takes care of your minor child.
- **Trustee**: The person who manages money in a trust for someone else.

You don't have to memorize all this—but you do need to know who's in charge of what when it comes to *your* life.

- Section 6: Pros and Cons of Updating Everything Now

You may be wondering: do I really need to tackle all of this at once?

Let's weigh it out:

- Pros:
- Full control over your financial and legal decisions.
- Prevents your ex or unwanted parties from being involved later.
- Makes your wishes crystal clear to others.
- Gives your children (or loved ones) a much smoother path if something happens to you.
- Cons:
- It takes time and effort.
- It may cost money to work with an attorney for new documents.
- Emotionally draining—revisiting hard conversations.
- Bottom Line:

It's worth it. You don't have to rush it all in one week, but you *do* need a plan and a timeline.

- Section 7: Action Steps – Protecting Your Present and Future

Let's break this down into clear, manageable tasks.

- Week 1: Health and Life Insurance
- Call current providers to check coverage and prices.
- Research options for health insurance if you lost coverage.
- Apply for life insurance or change the beneficiary on existing policies.
- Week 2: Property and Disability Insurance
- Update your auto policy and renters/homeowners insurance.

- Request disability insurance quotes if you're not covered by your job.
- Week 3: Legal Documents
- Review old documents and identify needed changes.
- Meet with an attorney to update your will, POAs, and guardianship preferences.
- Create or review a living will.
- Week 4: Organize and Store Safely
- Create a binder or digital vault with all insurance and legal documents.
- Share copies of key items (wills, POAs) with the people named in them.
- Schedule a calendar reminder to review policies yearly.

Section 8: Emotional Boundaries Around Insurance and Legal Documents

Let's talk about something that doesn't always get enough attention: the *emotional toll* of updating all this paperwork.

Because here's what no one tells you—when you're filling out forms, choosing beneficiaries, or naming new decision-makers, you're not just making financial decisions.

You're grieving.

You're grieving the fact that the person you once trusted with your life—your health, your children, your money—is no longer the person you'd choose. That hurts. Even if you wanted the divorce. Even if it was for the best.

This stuff is more than admin work. It's part of your healing process. It's acknowledgment. It's closure.

So give yourself permission to feel as you go:

- If you cry while removing your ex from your will, that's okay.
- If you feel angry when your ex refuses to carry life insurance for the kids, that's valid.
- If you feel overwhelmed by all the decisions, that's normal.

You are not being dramatic. You're being human.

So take breaks. Ask for help. And remember that protecting your future is not selfish—it's sacred.

Section 9: Real-Life Scenarios and What to Do

Let's walk through a few common situations divorced people face when it comes to protection:

Scenario 1: "I Lost My Health Insurance and Don't Know Where to Start."

Start with Healthcare.gov. You have 60 days from the date of divorce to enroll in a plan through the marketplace. Use the income calculator to see if you qualify for a subsidy. If your income is low, check your state's Medicaid guidelines.

Pro Tip: Some nonprofit hospitals offer free insurance navigators. Don't be afraid to ask for help.

Scenario 2: "My Ex Refuses to Carry Life Insurance, Even Though They Owe Child Support."

If life insurance was court-ordered in your divorce decree, you can go back to court to enforce it. If not, try to negotiate it during custody conversations. If that fails, consider purchasing a small policy on their life yourself (you'll need their consent and health info).

Pro Tip: Always make sure *you* own the policy if your ex is the insured.

Scenario 3: "I'm Naming My Sister as Power of Attorney, but We're Not Close."

This is a tough one. POA is a big responsibility. You want someone:

- Trustworthy
- Calm under pressure
- Willing to follow your wishes, even if it's hard

If your sister isn't the right fit, it's okay to name someone else—like a trusted friend or even a professional fiduciary.

Pro Tip: Whoever you choose, talk to them about your wishes in advance. Don't assume they'll "just know."

Scenario 4: "My Kids Are Minors—What Happens If I Die?"

If you have sole custody, you need to name a guardian in your will. If your ex is still living, they'll usually get custody unless they're proven unfit.

Still, your will can express your wishes clearly. You can also set up a trust so your kids receive money in stages (not all at 18) and name a trustee to manage it.

Pro Tip: The guardian and trustee don't have to be the same person. Sometimes that's better.

Section 10: How to Talk About This With Your Kids (Or Not)

This depends on their age, of course, but here are some guidelines:

For Young Kids:

Keep it simple. "I'm making sure everything is taken care of, just in case I ever get hurt or sick."

For Teens:

Be real. "Part of being a grown-up is getting things in order. I've updated some documents so if anything ever happened, you'd be protected."

For Adult Children:

Get specific. Share where documents are stored, who the decision-makers are, and how to access important info if needed.

Pro Tip: Don't wait until there's an emergency. Have the talk now—then you can relax.

Section 11: Legacy Isn't Just for the Wealthy

Even if you don't think you have a lot of money, you still have a legacy. You have a story. A name. A memory that lives on in your kids, your friends, your community.

Wills and insurance aren't about being rich. They're about being responsible.

Ask yourself:

- What do I want my kids to remember about how I handled life after divorce?
- How do I want to be remembered when I'm gone?
- What lessons about preparation and self-respect do I want to pass down?

This is your chance to show them what resilience looks like in real life.

Final Encouragement: You Are Not Being Morbid—You Are Being Wise

Filling out legal documents. Buying life insurance. Naming someone to make decisions for you if you can't.

It might feel grim at first.

But let's flip the perspective. You're not planning for your end—you're protecting your beginning.

You're giving yourself and your loved ones the gift of *certainty* in a world that can feel uncertain.

And you don't have to do it alone. Ask your financial advisor, estate attorney, or even your therapist to walk you through it. You are allowed to need help. You are allowed to take your time.

But what you are not allowed to do anymore? Ignore your power.

A Gentle Nudge to Close Out This Chapter

The hardest part of starting over is believing that you're worth protecting.

But you are.

You are worth the paperwork. The policies. The signatures. The preparation.

You are worth being remembered with love and dignity—not legal confusion.

You are worth the peace of knowing your children, your assets, and your wishes are safe and secure.

You are worth every ounce of strength and wisdom you've poured into this new chapter.

And you are not doing it alone—not anymore.

Chapter 22: Investing After Divorce – Starting Small, Building Smart

This Isn't About Wall Street—It's About Your Street

If you've made it this far in the book, you've already rebuilt the foundation. You've opened new accounts. You've updated your insurance. You've taken legal control of your life. But now it's time to do more than protect. It's time to *build.*

This chapter is about investing—not in some cold, jargon-filled, TV-screaming-stock-picking kind of way. We're not going to talk to you like a hedge fund manager. We're going to talk to you like someone who's rebuilding after heartbreak, exhaustion, and maybe financial trauma. Someone who's ready to take control, but quietly wondering:

"Where do I even begin?"

Right here. Right now. You don't need to know everything. You just need to take the first step. Investing after divorce doesn't mean you need to be rich or have a fancy financial advisor. It means making sure your money works for you—so you don't have to work forever.

It means building a future where you're not just surviving on a budget—you're growing wealth, building freedom, and redefining what success looks like... for you.

Let's do this together.

Why Investing Matters (Especially Now)

Divorce often hits women harder financially—but this chapter is for everyone. Whether your finances were shattered, split, or simply stretched during the divorce, now is your moment to make intentional, empowering choices with whatever you have left.

What Investing Isn't:

- A get-rich-quick scheme
- A game only "smart people" or "finance bros" play
- Something to be afraid of

What Investing Is:

- A tool to build wealth over time
- A way to protect your money from inflation and loss of purchasing power
- A vote for your future goals, one dollar at a time

It's okay if you don't know much right now. That's why this chapter exists—to take you by the hand and walk you into this with clarity and calm.

The Emotional Side of Investing After Divorce

Let's get this out of the way: investing isn't just about numbers—it's about *trust.*

And after a divorce? Trust can feel scarce. Maybe your ex handled the investing. Maybe you ignored it for years. Maybe the thought of risking *anything* makes your stomach tighten.

That's normal.

You've already been through enough unpredictability. The last thing you want is to make another mistake. But not investing can be a bigger mistake in the long run—because it's not just about growing money. It's about *owning your future.*

You are no longer in survival mode. You're in building mode.

So let's build smart.

Step One: Know the Ground You're Standing On

Before we can invest, we need to understand what we're working with.

Questions to Ask Yourself:

- What's my current income?
- What are my fixed and variable expenses?
- What's left over each month after necessities?
- Do I have an emergency fund (at least 3–6 months of expenses)?
- Do I have any high-interest debt (credit cards, payday loans)?

If you're still in the process of stabilizing your cash flow or paying down high-interest debt, you may want to start small—or pause and return to investing once you're on firmer ground. That's not failure. That's *strategy.*

Step Two: Learn the Language Without the Intimidation

You don't need a finance degree to be a smart investor. But you do need to understand some basics.

Investing Terms in Plain English:

- **Stock**: A share of ownership in a company. If the company does well, your investment can grow.
- **Bond**: A loan you give to a company or government. They pay you back with interest.
- **Mutual Fund**: A collection of stocks or bonds managed by profession-

als.

- **ETF (Exchange-Traded Fund)**: Like a mutual fund, but traded like a stock. Often lower fees.
- **Index Fund**: A type of fund that follows a whole market, like the S&P 500.
- **Diversification**: Spreading your investments across different types so you're not putting all your eggs in one basket.
- **Risk Tolerance**: Your personal comfort with how much your investments might go up and down.

You don't have to memorize all of this now. We'll revisit these terms as we go.

Step Three: Choose Where to Start – Even $50 Is Enough

You Do Not Need Thousands to Invest

One of the biggest myths in investing is that you need a big lump sum. You don't. You can start with $5, $25, or $100 per month.

What matters is consistency.

Here are three beginner-friendly ways to start:

1. Employer Retirement Plan (401(k) or 403(b))

- If you have access to one, especially with matching contributions, use it.
- You can usually start with 1%–3% of your paycheck.
- Contributions are often pre-tax, which lowers your taxable income.

Pros: Easy to set up, often matched by employer, automatic. **Cons**: Limited fund choices, penalties for early withdrawal before age 59½.

2. Roth IRA or Traditional IRA

- Individual Retirement Accounts you can open on your own.
- Roth = pay taxes now, withdraw tax-free later.
- Traditional = tax break now, pay taxes when you retire.

Pros: More control over investments, flexible. **Cons**: Income limits on Roth IRAs; penalties for early withdrawals.

3. Investment Apps (Betterment, Fidelity, Schwab, Acorns, etc.)

- Many let you start with $0–$5.
- Some round up spare change from purchases and invest it automatically.

Pros: Super easy to use, educational tools built-in. **Cons**: May have fees, and not all apps are equal—do your research.

Step Four: Build a Portfolio You Can Sleep With

Let's talk about what to invest *in*. Because throwing money into "the market" without a plan is like walking into a gym and lifting random weights without knowing what muscles you're working.

Your investment portfolio—the collection of your investments—should reflect three things:

1. **Your goals**
2. **Your timeline**
3. **Your risk tolerance**

Common Portfolio Types:

The Conservative Starter

- 60% Bonds
- 30% Large Cap Stocks (like S&P 500)
- 10% Cash or Money Market Funds

Great for: Someone easing in, still regaining confidence, or needing access to funds in the near future.

The Balanced Builder

- 50% Stock Funds (mix of U.S. and international)
- 40% Bonds
- 10% Real Estate or Alternatives

Great for: Someone with 5–10+ years until retirement, moderate risk tolerance, and a steady income.

The Growth-Focused Investor

- 80% Stock Funds (diversified across sectors and geography)
- 15% Bonds
- 5% Alternatives or Real Estate

Great for: Long-term investors, higher risk tolerance, or younger divorcees rebuilding with time on their side.

You don't need to choose the perfect mix on Day 1. Most apps and brokerage firms will help you build a starter portfolio based on a simple quiz.

Pro Tip: Choose simplicity over complexity. Index funds and ETFs are your best friends when starting out.

Step Five: Automate and Forget (But Check In Quarterly)

You've been through enough stress. Don't add investing to your plate in a way that feels overwhelming. Automation is the antidote to anxiety.

How to Automate Your Investing:

- Set up automatic transfers from your checking account to your investment account.
- Start with a small amount: $25 or $50 monthly is fine.
- Increase by 1–2% each year, or every time you get a raise.

Then let it grow. Review quarterly—not daily.

Think of it like planting a garden. You don't dig up the seeds every day to see if they've sprouted. You water it, protect it, and trust the process.

Step Six: Avoid Common Mistakes (Especially Post-Divorce)

1. Investing Before You're Ready

- Don't invest if you don't have an emergency fund or you're drowning in debt.
- Start with a solid foundation.

2. Falling for Trends

- Crypto, meme stocks, NFTs—if it sounds too good to be true, it is.
- Stick with diversified, long-term investing strategies.

3. Letting Fear Freeze You

- "What if I lose everything?" is a valid fear. But inflation guarantees that cash alone *will* lose value over time.
- The market goes up and down, but historically grows over time.

4. Not Updating Beneficiaries

- Make sure your ex is *not* still the beneficiary on your retirement or brokerage accounts (unless that's court-ordered).
- Update all beneficiaries ASAP.

Step Seven: Learn From Others – Case Studies of Rebuilding Wealth

Amanda, 47 – "I Didn't Even Know What a Roth IRA Was"

Amanda hadn't made a single financial decision during her 18-year marriage. Post-divorce, she started attending free online finance workshops. She opened a Roth IRA with just $100. Within a year, she had automated monthly contributions of $150 and learned how to pick simple index funds. Now she manages her own portfolio and says it makes her feel "like a boss."

Dion, 55 – "I Lost Half in the Divorce. But I'm Gaining It Back"

Dion split everything down the middle in a high-asset divorce. But he walked away without a financial plan. He met with a financial coach, set a new retirement target, and started maxing out his 401(k) contributions. Now, five years later, he's within reach of his retirement goals. "I used to think I was too old to rebuild. Now I know it's never too late."

Jasmin, 39 – "I Invested to Prove I Could Do It"

Jasmin was told for years she "wasn't good with money." After the divorce, she took a different approach. She started with $5 on an app just to prove she could understand it. Then she bought a personal finance book, opened a Roth IRA, and began investing monthly. "It's not just about money—it's about belief. Investing taught me to bet on myself."

Step Eight: Align Your Investments With Your Values

After a divorce, it's common to want everything in your life to reflect *you*. That includes your money.

Did you know you can invest in companies that align with your values?

Socially Responsible Investing (SRI)

- Avoids companies involved in tobacco, weapons, or pollution.
- Focuses on companies with good environmental, social, and governance practices.

Faith-Based Investing

- Aligns with religious values and screens out certain industries.

Green Funds

- Focus on clean energy and sustainability.

Ask your advisor or use screeners on platforms like Morningstar, Fidelity, or Betterment to find funds that match your principles.

Step Nine: Reinvest in Yourself Along the Way

You are your greatest asset.

While investing in the stock market is important, so is investing in *you*. After a divorce, it's easy to feel like your best years—financially or otherwise—are behind you. But that's a lie. Your earning potential, your skills, your wisdom—they can all grow from here.

Ways to Reinvest in Yourself:

- Take a course in a skill you've always wanted to master.
- Go back to school if it makes sense for your career goals.
- Work with a career coach to negotiate a raise or change industries.
- Start a side hustle you've always dreamed about.

Pro Tip: Use part of your monthly "investment" budget to develop yourself. Your income potential is one of the best returns you'll ever see.

Step Ten: Create an Investing Ritual

Money is emotional. Divorce is emotional. Investing, if done right, can be healing. It's a way of saying, "I believe in my future."

That's why I recommend creating an investing ritual. A simple, grounding practice you do monthly to stay engaged with your money, not intimidated by it.

Your Monthly Investing Ritual:

- Log in to your account.
- Review your balance.
- Check your contributions.
- Celebrate small wins ("I invested $25 this month—that's *everything*.")
- Journal your thoughts: "How did investing make me feel this month?"

This turns investing from a cold, distant task into an act of care and confidence.

Step Eleven: Talk to a Professional—But Only If They Respect You

If you decide to work with a financial advisor or planner, that's great. But choose someone who:

- Listens more than they talk
- Doesn't make you feel stupid for asking basic questions
- Charges in a transparent way (fee-only is often best)
- Doesn't pressure you to buy products you don't understand

Red Flags:

- "Guaranteed returns"
- Unclear fees or commissions
- Glossing over your questions
- Talking over you or minimizing your goals

This is *your* money, *your* future. You deserve respect, not just results.

Quick Investing Checklist: Your First 90 Days

Here's a simple timeline to take action in manageable steps:

Month 1:

- Assess your budget and emergency fund
- Learn the basic investing terms
- Choose a platform (401(k), IRA, or app)

Month 2:

- Open an account
- Set up auto-contributions (even just $25/month)
- Pick simple, diversified investments (index or target date funds)

Month 3:

- Review your performance (no stress—just check in)
- Revisit your goals
- Increase your contributions by 1–2% if possible

Keep this cycle going every 90 days. Review. Reflect. Recommit.

Final Reflection: What You're Really Investing In

You might think you're investing in stocks.

You're not.

You're investing in:

- Freedom from fear
- The ability to rest without anxiety
- Your children's future
- Your next chapter, whatever you want it to be
- The version of you who knows she (or he) can do this

Divorce stripped away the old financial safety net—but it gave you the chance to build one that's stronger. One made of knowledge, clarity, and empowerment. One that reflects *you*, not your former life.

Let every dollar you invest whisper: "I'm not afraid anymore."

Final Encouragement: You Are Already an Investor

If you made it through this chapter, you've already started.

You invested your time. You invested your attention. You invested your *hope.*

And hope is the most powerful capital there is.

This isn't about how much you have. It's about how consistently you show up.

You are not too late. You are not too old. You are not too behind. You are ready.

So whether you're investing $5 or $500 this month, remember: this isn't just about the stock market. It's about building a life that's rooted in belief. In balance. In you.

The market will rise and fall. But your commitment? That's where real growth starts.

Section 1: Investment Readiness Quiz

Instructions: Answer each question honestly. There are no right or wrong answers—this is just to assess where you are right now.

1. Do you currently have an emergency fund of at least 3 months of living expenses?

- ☐ Yes
- ☐ No
- ☐ I'm working on it

1. Are you carrying any high-interest debt (like credit cards)?

- ☐ Yes
- ☐ No

1. Do you know your monthly income and expenses?

- ☐ Yes
- ☐ No
- ☐ Kind of—I'm still figuring it out

1. Have you ever invested before (outside of a retirement plan)?

- ☐ Yes
- ☐ No
- ☐ I'm not sure

1. How do you feel when you think about investing?

- ☐ Calm and curious
- ☐ Anxious and overwhelmed
- ☐ Avoidant—it feels like too much

Scoring:

- If you answered mostly "Yes" or "Calm and curious": You're likely ready to start investing now.
- If you answered "No" to emergency fund or carry high-interest debt: Focus on stabilizing before investing.
- If you're somewhere in between: Start small and educate yourself as you go.

Section 2: SMART Goals Tracker

Instructions: Use this template to create clear, actionable investing goals.

S – Specific: What exactly do you want to achieve? Example: "I want to invest $50/month into a Roth IRA."

M – Measurable: How will you track progress? Example: "I'll check my balance every month and increase contributions by $10 quarterly."

A – Achievable: Is this realistic based on your income and expenses? Example: "Yes, I can afford $50/month without sacrificing essentials."

R – Relevant: Why does this matter to you? Example: "Because I want to retire without depending on anyone else."

T – Time-Bound: What's your timeline? Example: "I'll contribute consistently for 12 months, then reassess."

Your Goal:

S: ____
_

M: ____
__

A: ____
__

R: ____
__

T: ____
__

Section 3: Monthly Contribution Planner

Instructions: Use this worksheet to decide what amount you can comfortably invest monthly. Start small if needed.

Step 1: Know What You Spend

- Monthly Income: $__________
- Essential Expenses: $__________
- Emergency Fund (Y/N): ________

Step 2: Decide Your Monthly Contribution

- Start with a small amount: $__________
- Add a reminder: (Circle one) Weekly / Biweekly / Monthly

Step 3: Plan to Increase Later

- Increase goal: $__________ by (date) ________________

Remember: Consistency is more powerful than size. Even $25/month is powerful over time.

Section 4: Sample "Divorcee's First Investment Portfolio"

Risk Profile: Moderate risk, long-term growth, simple to manage

Ideal For: Someone starting over post-divorce, ages 30–60, with a long-term mindset

Portfolio Breakdown:

- 40% U.S. Total Stock Market Index Fund (e.g., VTI or FSKAX)
- 20% International Stock Market Index Fund (e.g., VXUS or IXUS)
- 30% Total Bond Market Fund (e.g., BND or AGG)
- 10% High-Yield Savings or Money Market Fund

Where to Build This:

- Roth IRA or Traditional IRA at Vanguard, Fidelity, or Schwab
- Robo-advisors like Betterment or Wealthfront
- Apps like M1 Finance or SoFi Invest

Rebalance: Once a year or if your allocations drift by more than 5%

Note: If this feels overwhelming, consider a Target Date Fund (e.g., "Target 2045"), which rebalances for you.

Section 5: Quarterly Investing Reflection Worksheet

Instructions: Complete this every 3 months to stay engaged and assess your progress.

Date: _______________

1. How much did I invest this quarter? $__________
2. How consistent was I with contributions?

- ☐ Always
- ☐ Most of the time
- ☐ I missed a few
- ☐ I didn't contribute

1. How do I feel about my investments right now?
2.
3. What is one thing I learned about money or investing this quarter?
4.
5. What's one thing I'll adjust for the next quarter?

Section 6: Beginner Investing Glossary

Use this as a reference as you read and invest:

- **Asset Allocation**: The mix of different types of investments in your portfolio.
- **Diversification**: Spreading your money across many investments to reduce risk.
- **Index Fund**: A fund that tracks a market index (like the S&P 500).
- **ETF**: A type of fund that can be traded like a stock.
- **Rebalancing**: Adjusting your portfolio to return to your original allocation.
- **Risk Tolerance**: Your ability and willingness to handle ups and downs

in the market.

- **Compound Interest**: Earning interest on your interest over time—how money grows exponentially.

Chapter 23: Career Transitions, Re-entering the Workforce, or Going Back to School

You're Not Starting Over—You're Starting Differently

Let's begin with this truth: You are not too old. It is not too late. And you are not behind.

You're just in a different place. A place where you're finally asking: *Now that I've survived this chapter of my life, how do I build something new that actually fits who I am today?*

Maybe you took time off to raise kids. Maybe your ex made more money and your career took a back seat. Maybe your industry changed while your life fell apart. Or maybe—just maybe—you've realized that what you were doing before was never really what you wanted.

Wherever you are, this chapter is for you.

It's about rediscovering your financial independence, your confidence, and your professional worth. Whether that means changing careers, re-entering the workforce after a long break, starting a business, or enrolling in school, we're going to walk through every step with steady hands and real talk.

This isn't just about making money. It's about making a life that works—on your terms.

Why This Step Feels So Big

You've been through a major life shift. Divorce doesn't just break hearts—it can break routines, identities, support systems, and self-esteem. So when you're thinking about work or school again, you might feel:

- Nervous about your skills
- Embarrassed about your résumé gap
- Overwhelmed by technology or changing job markets
- Tired. Just… tired.

That's okay. That's normal. This is emotional work as much as financial.

But here's what else is true: You've already done hard things. You've adapted. You've stretched. You've made impossible choices and lived to tell about it.

So this? This is doable. One step at a time.

Section 1: Re-Entering the Workforce

Let's start with the basics. You were in the workforce, then you weren't. Now you're ready to return—but everything feels different.

Maybe it's been five years. Maybe it's been fifteen. Doesn't matter. What matters is that you're ready to move forward.

Common Roadblocks:

- "I don't know what I'm good at anymore."
- "My skills feel outdated."
- "Who's going to hire someone with a gap like mine?"
- "I can't afford childcare, so what's the point?"

Let's break these down.

Truths You Need to Hear:

- Skills don't disappear—they just need dusting off.
- Soft skills (communication, resilience, organization) are in high demand.
- Employers are increasingly open to non-traditional candidates.
- The best job for you now may not be the one you had before—and that's okay.

Section 2: First Step – Take Inventory

Before you apply to a single job, we're going to pause and take stock.

What to Write Down:

- Every paid or unpaid job you've ever done (yes, including parenting, volunteering, caregiving).
- Skills you used or learned in those roles.
- What you liked—and what you hated.
- What hours, environments, and work styles you thrive in.

Skills That Count (Even If You Didn't Get Paid For Them):

- Scheduling and logistics (kids, caregiving, household)
- Budgeting, bill management, financial planning
- Conflict resolution, negotiation
- Writing, communication, emails, tech tools
- Emotional intelligence (managing stress, motivating others)

Pro Tip: Don't underestimate what you've done outside the office. Life experience is a résumé in itself.

Section 3: Reskilling and Upskilling

The job market has changed. But that's not a threat—it's an opportunity.

Ways to Learn Without Going Broke:

- **Online Platforms**: Coursera, LinkedIn Learning, edX, Skillshare
- **Community Colleges**: Affordable, local, practical
- **Workforce Development Centers**: Often free or subsidized
- **Apprenticeships/Internships**: Earn while you learn
- **Library Workshops & Career Events**: Free and community-based

Popular, Flexible Career Fields Post-Divorce:

- Healthcare (nursing, phlebotomy, billing)
- Tech (UX design, customer success, data entry, cybersecurity)
- Education (paraeducator, substitute, online tutoring)
- Remote roles (admin, writing, customer service)
- Skilled trades (electrical, plumbing, HVAC—yes, women too!)

Section 4: Resume Gaps and Reinvention – The Truth About Hiring Today

Let's talk about the elephant in the room: the gap.

Whether it's 2 years or 20, that break in your resume is not a deal-breaker. The narrative around "employment gaps" has changed—especially after the pandemic, where caregiving and career shifts became the norm.

What You Don't Need to Do:

- Apologize for your gap
- Pretend it didn't happen
- Downplay your non-paid experience

What You Do Need to Do:

- Own your story with confidence
- Frame your time off as intentional growth or responsibility
- Highlight the transferable skills you've gained

Example:

> *"Took time to raise children and manage household logistics. Developed advanced scheduling, budget management, and negotiation skills while coordinating activities, appointments, and education. Now re-entering the workforce with fresh perspective, high adaptability, and readiness to contribute."*

That's not weakness. That's *real life*.

Section 5: Your Return-to-Work Toolkit

Here's what you'll need as you step back into the workforce:

1. **Updated Resume**

- Focus on skills, not just job titles.
- Use active verbs: managed, organized, created, supported.
- Include unpaid work if it shows relevant experience.

1. **Professional Email Address**

- Keep it simple (e.g., yourname@gmail.com).
- No nicknames or outdated domains like AOL or Hotmail.

1. **LinkedIn Profile**

- Create one if you haven't already.
- Use your headline to tell people what you do now or what you're aiming for.
- Connect with former coworkers, classmates, or mentors.

1. **Interview Practice**

- Prepare a short "career story" that explains your past, your gap, and what you're seeking now.
- Rehearse common questions with a friend or coach.

1. **Work Attire**

- Don't overspend. Just one or two updated outfits that make you feel confident will do.

Section 6: Considering a Career Pivot

After divorce, many people realize they don't want to go back to what they were doing before.

That job may not fit your life anymore. It may not pay enough. It may not align with the version of yourself that's emerging.

And that's okay.

How to Explore a Career Pivot:

- Talk to people in roles that interest you (informational interviews)
- Shadow a professional for a day
- Take a weekend or online course to test interest
- Attend networking events or industry webinars
- Look at job descriptions—what appeals to you?

A pivot doesn't mean starting from scratch. It means building on what you already know in a new direction.

Section 7: Starting a Business or Side Hustle

Sometimes going back to work isn't about applying for a job—it's about creating one.

If you've ever thought about starting your own business, now might be the time.

Pros:

- Flexibility (especially if you're managing custody or care responsibilities)
- Creative control
- Potential to scale income

Cons:

- Inconsistent income at first
- Requires self-motivation and planning
- May take time to be profitable

Common Post-Divorce Side Hustles:

- Virtual assistant or freelance admin
- Etsy shops (crafts, printables, digital art)
- Tutoring or teaching online
- Pet sitting, house cleaning, childcare
- Consulting in your former field

Start small. Keep your day job if needed. And let your hustle grow as you do.

Section 8: Going Back to School – What You Need to Know

Education can be a powerful way to reclaim your confidence and earning potential—but it's also a financial decision.

Before You Enroll:

- Research accredited programs
- Compare tuition and ROI (will this degree increase your income?)
- Look into flexible formats (part-time, night classes, online)
- Understand financial aid (grants, scholarships, work-study)

Federal Aid Options:

- Fill out the FAFSA to access loans, grants, and scholarships
- Look for scholarships specifically for women returning to school or single parents

Smart School Paths:

- Associate degree in healthcare, technology, or trades
- Certificate programs in bookkeeping, coding, medical billing
- Bachelor's completion programs for adults
- Non-degree continuing ed or bootcamps

Section 9: Financial Planning for Work or School

Whether you're returning to work, launching a side business, or going back to school, your finances will shift. Let's build a plan that keeps you grounded while you grow.

1. Build a Transition Budget

Create a "bridge budget" for the next 6–12 months that reflects:

- Reduced income during school or job search
- New expenses (childcare, transportation, tuition)
- Any temporary financial aid, grants, or part-time income

2. Plan for the Pay Gap

When re-entering, your starting salary may be lower than expected. That's okay. You're not stuck. Use this as a stepping stone, not a stopping point.

Pro Tip: Focus on companies that offer benefits (healthcare, retirement matching, education reimbursement). The value goes beyond salary.

3. Track Income Changes

If you're freelancing, working part-time, or building a side hustle, your income may be irregular. Use tools like:

- YNAB (You Need A Budget)
- Tiller (for spreadsheet lovers)
- A simple Google Sheet to track monthly cash flow

Section 10: Dealing With Imposter Syndrome

Whether you're 29 or 59, you might hear a voice in your head whispering:

- "You're not qualified."
- "You're too old."
- "They'll laugh at your resume."
- "You've been out of the game too long."

That voice is a liar.

Imposter syndrome thrives in moments of transition. It feeds off fear. But here's the truth: You belong. You have value. You bring perspective that a 22-year-old straight out of school simply can't.

Own your voice. Own your experience. Walk in the room like you've been through something—because you have. And that makes you powerful.

Section 11: Real-Life Transitions – Stories of Reinvention

Melissa, 41 – "I Went from PTA to Payroll Administrator"

After 12 years as a stay-at-home mom, Melissa enrolled in a 6-month bookkeeping course through her local community college. With help from a career center, she landed a remote job doing payroll for a nonprofit. She works 30 hours a week and is saving for her own home.

Renée, 50 – "Divorce Made Me Finally Write My Book"

Renée had worked in marketing but stepped away to raise her kids. After divorce, she started freelance writing—then wrote her first e-book. She now runs a coaching business for other women writing books in midlife.

James, 38 – "I Was a Chef. Now I Teach Culinary Arts"

James had custody of his two kids and couldn't keep up with the late nights. He went back to school for a teaching credential and now works at a vocational high school. "It's not less than—it's just different. And that's enough."

Section 12: Building Your Confidence Muscle

Confidence isn't something you either have or don't. It's something you *build*—like a muscle. And after divorce, that muscle might feel weak. But it's still there. It just needs reps.

How to Strengthen It:

- Say "yes" to one new opportunity a month (job fair, info session, interview).
- Practice talking about yourself—out loud, not just in your head.
- Write a "brag file": a running list of your wins, compliments, and moments you showed up strong.
- Surround yourself with people who speak to your future, not your past.

Your resume might have gaps, but your value doesn't.

Section 13: Career Transition Action Plan – 30/60/90 Days

First 30 Days:

- Update your resume and LinkedIn
- Make a list of skills you need to refresh or build
- Start applying to 3 jobs a week or researching programs

Next 60 Days:

- Enroll in a short course or attend a workshop
- Schedule two informational interviews
- Create a simple budget for job-search or school transition

Day 90 and Beyond:

- Apply to at least one job a week or submit your school application
- Join a professional group or online forum in your new field
- Celebrate progress—even if it's slow

Final Encouragement: You Are Not Broken—You're Becoming

This chapter wasn't about going back—it's about moving forward.

You're not reclaiming an old life. You're creating a new one. One with boundaries, bravery, and belief in your own damn brilliance.

If you're applying for jobs through tears, starting a business with fear in your throat, or walking into a classroom with shaky hands—you're still doing it. And that matters more than perfection.

This is not just career planning. This is reclaiming your voice. Your independence. Your next chapter.

So give yourself credit. Then give yourself a deadline. Then give yourself a chance.

You've already survived the hard part. Now it's time to rise.

Chapter 25: Co-Parenting and Finances – Navigating Shared Costs Respectfully

Love Your Kids More Than You Hate Your Ex

Let's start with the hardest truth right up front.

Co-parenting is hard. Co-parenting with money involved? Even harder.

You're navigating two households, two perspectives, two incomes, two calendars—and one set of kids who didn't ask for any of it. And somehow, you have to keep it together for their sake while also rebuilding your own financial life.

This chapter isn't going to sugarcoat the difficulty. But it *is* going to give you tools. Language. Structure. Scripts. Strategies. And maybe even a little peace.

Because when it comes to money and co-parenting, the goal isn't perfection. The goal is respect, reliability, and putting your kids first—even if your relationship with your co-parent is strained, messy, or complicated.

This is for you, the parent who's doing their best. The one who's tired of arguing. The one who's scared to bring up child support again. The one who feels stuck between protecting their kids and protecting their peace.

Let's walk this one out—together.

Why Financial Co-Parenting Feels So Personal

Let's name what's underneath the surface.

Money and parenting are deeply emotional. You're not just splitting bills—you're splitting values, priorities, and sometimes even visions for your child's future.

You may be asking:

- "Why should I pay for private school when they barely see their kid?"
- "Why do they get to spoil them while I pay for the basics?"

- "Why can't we just agree on what's important?"

These are valid questions. But they're also *traps* if you don't have a framework to manage them.

Because under the resentment, fear, and frustration is a very real need: to create stability for your child. And that starts with respectful, consistent, clear communication about money.

Section 1: Understanding the Legal and Emotional Framework

What the Court Covers (and What It Doesn't)

Your custody agreement may outline child support, custody schedules, and major decision-making authority. But here's the thing—**it's often vague or incomplete when it comes to shared expenses.**

Typically covered by child support:

- Housing, food, clothing
- Basic medical and dental

Often not covered (but still necessary):

- Daycare and after-school programs
- Sports, dance, and extracurriculars
- School trips, yearbooks, activity fees
- Tutoring or special needs services
- Summer camps, travel, college savings

That's where respectful co-parenting conversations matter most—because the court can't plan for every birthday party, new backpack, or emergency root canal.

Section 2: Building a Financial Co-Parenting Plan

If your co-parenting relationship is civil enough for collaboration, here's how to build a shared expense plan that works.

Step 1: Define Shared Expenses

Make a list of what's considered "shared" versus "individual." Agree on:

- What gets split 50/50
- What is each parent's responsibility
- What requires pre-approval before spending

Step 2: Set a Communication Method

Use one consistent platform or tool. Options include:

- Co-parenting apps like OurFamilyWizard, Coparently, or TalkingParents
- Shared Google Docs or Sheets
- Email summaries

Pro Tip: Keep all money-related communication clear, calm, and documented.

Step 3: Agree on a Payment Process

- Will you each pay vendors directly?
- Will one person pay and request reimbursement?
- How often will you reconcile shared costs—monthly, quarterly?

The clearer your process, the fewer the fights.

Section 3: Scripts for Difficult Money Conversations

Sometimes you need the words before you find the peace. Here are some conversation openers you can adapt:

1. **"Hey, I'd love to get on the same page about school supplies and fall activities. Can we agree on a budget together?"**
2. **"I want to make sure we're both contributing fairly to things outside child support. Can we talk through a system that works for both of us?"**
3. **"I noticed I've been covering more of the medical co-pays lately. Can we review how we're handling those going forward?"**

These aren't always easy. But they're easier than bottling resentment or escalating tension.

Section 4: When Communication Is Difficult or Toxic

Not every co-parenting relationship is healthy. Some are marked by avoidance, defensiveness, control, or even financial manipulation. If that's your situation, you're not alone—and you're not powerless.

Strategies for High-Conflict Co-Parenting:

1. **Document Everything** Keep a written record of every shared expense, request, and response. Use email or co-parenting apps with time-stamped communication logs.
2. **Avoid Emotional Language** Stick to facts and numbers. Keep messages short, clear, and non-confrontational.

Instead of:

> *"You never pay your fair share. I'm tired of chasing you."*

Try:

> *"Here's the invoice for Ella's soccer fees. Please reimburse $75 by the 10th as agreed."*

3. Set Boundaries You do not have to explain every financial decision. You can say:

> *"This is something I'm choosing to cover. I'm not requesting reimbursement."*

4. Use Third Parties In cases of extreme conflict, consider:

- Family court mediator
- Parenting coordinator
- Financial neutral (used in collaborative divorce)
- A trusted mutual contact (for handoffs or documentation)

Section 5: The Emotional Toll of Unequal Contributions

Let's talk about the feelings that come up when one parent is contributing more—financially, emotionally, or both.

Common Feelings:

- Resentment: "Why am I always the one paying for everything?"
- Guilt: "I can't afford what they can."
- Insecurity: "Will my kids think I care less because I have less?"
- Burnout: "I'm holding it all together, and it's exhausting."

These feelings are real. And they deserve space. But they don't have to dictate your behavior.

What You Can Do:

- Focus on what you *can* give—your consistency, your presence, your effort.
- Reassure your kids through quality time, not quantity of gifts.
- Don't compete. You're not in a contest—you're in a commitment to raise good humans.

You don't have to match your ex dollar for dollar. You just have to show up with love, accountability, and intention.

Section 6: Planning for the Big Stuff (Even When You Disagree)

Kids don't stay little forever. And sooner than you think, they'll be talking about:

- Cars
- Proms
- College
- Weddings

These milestones often cause conflict because they're expensive, emotional, and sometimes unexpected.

Start Early, Even If It's Awkward

> *"Have you thought about what we'll do when she starts looking at colleges?" "Would you be open to starting a savings plan, even if it's small?" "Can we agree on a cap for big expenses like senior trips or braces?"*

If You Can't Agree

Do what you can independently. Open a 529 college savings account. Invite grandparents to contribute for birthdays. Look into financial aid or grants.

You don't need mutual agreement to start building a financial future for your kids.

Section 7: Tools and Apps That Can Help

Here are some tools that can help streamline financial co-parenting:

Co-Parenting Apps:

- **OurFamilyWizard**: Expense tracking, communication, calendar, reimbursements
- **Coparently**: Shared costs, calendar, messaging
- **TalkingParents**: Court-admissible message records

Payment Tools:

- **Zelle, Venmo, CashApp**: Fast reimbursement (just keep screenshots)
- **Splitwise**: Shared cost tracking and repayment reminders

Budgeting Tools:

- **Mint or YNAB**: Track your own finances
- **Google Sheets**: Custom cost tracker for recurring shared expenses

Section 8: Creating a Co-Parenting Financial Agreement

Even if the court didn't mandate it, you can still create your own informal agreement. Here's a basic structure to follow:

Co-Parenting Financial Agreement Outline:

1. **List of Shared Expenses**
2. (e.g., school, medical, sports, gifts)
3. **Split Percentages**
4. (50/50 or based on income disparity)
5. **Payment Method and Timeline**
6. (e.g., reimburse by the 10th of the following month)
7. **Approval Process for New Expenses**
8. (e.g., "All new costs over $100 require pre-approval by both parties.")
9. **Review Schedule**
10. (e.g., "We'll review this agreement every 6 months.")
11. **Conflict Resolution Plan**
12. (e.g., "We'll mediate unresolved issues through [insert agreed person/app/lawyer].")

Put it in writing. Sign it. Refer back when needed.

Section 9: Teaching Kids About Money Without Undermining Each Other

One of the hardest parts of co-parenting is modeling consistency when the financial philosophies between homes are completely different.

Maybe your ex is the "buy it all, spoil them silly" parent. Or maybe they're the opposite—rigid, controlling, and obsessed with saving every penny. Either way, your child is watching—and learning.

You Can't Control Their House, But You Can Own Your Influence

Here's how to teach your kids healthy money values, even in a divided home:

1. **Speak from Your Values, Not Your Bitterness**

Instead of, "Your dad never budgets," say:

> *"In this house, we plan where our money goes so we can take care of what matters most."*

2. Be Honest Without Oversharing

You don't need to share legal details or child support disputes. But you *can* say:

> *"Mom and Dad have different ways of doing things, and that's okay. This is how I handle money here."*

3. Involve Them in Real-Life Decisions

Give older kids a budget for back-to-school shopping. Let younger ones help meal plan. Let them *see* how thoughtful money management works.

4. Celebrate Their Emotional Wins

If they choose to save instead of spend, praise that. If they offer to use their allowance for something shared, acknowledge the maturity.

Kids can thrive in co-parenting homes when they have at least one parent showing them what financial wisdom, calm, and care look like in action.

Section 10: Real-Life Co-Parenting Stories

Tasha, 38 – "We Use an App for Everything"

Tasha and her ex were cordial but distant. After one too many late reimbursements, they agreed to use OurFamilyWizard. "It changed everything. Now there's no emotion, just facts. It feels less personal—which is exactly what I needed."

Juan, 42 – "We Had to Start Over After a Big Fight"

Juan's ex was always late on her share of daycare costs. It caused tension at every pickup. Eventually, he asked her to sit down with a neutral third party (a family therapist) and rework their financial plan. "We still don't agree on everything—but we have structure now."

Lisa, 34 – "I Cover More Than I Should—But I Budget For It"

Lisa's co-parent hasn't contributed to anything outside of court-ordered child support. "It's frustrating, but I budget knowing I'll likely carry more. I've stopped fighting over every receipt. I focus on what my son needs and give myself grace."

Section 11: Financial Red Flags to Watch For in Co-Parenting

Not all co-parents are acting in good faith. Here are red flags that might indicate manipulation or financial abuse:

- **Refusing to pay agreed-upon costs but still spending lavishly elsewhere**
- **Deliberately missing payments to "punish" you**
- **Using money as leverage to change custody arrangements**
- **Pressuring you to cover everything to maintain "peace"**
- **Withholding reimbursements or making you beg**

If this is happening, document everything and consider seeking legal guidance. Financial abuse is real—and you do not have to accept it to "keep the peace."

Section 12: Co-Parenting Financial Affirmations

Because some days, you just need a reminder. Here are a few truths to keep on repeat:

- I can't control what my co-parent does, but I can control how I show up.
- I lead with respect, even if it's not always returned.
- My kids will remember how I made them feel—not what I could afford.
- I am building financial stability for my family, one decision at a time.
- I protect my peace and my power.

Write your own affirmations and post them on your mirror, your fridge, your phone wallpaper—wherever you need a reminder that you're doing just fine.

Section 13: 30/60/90 Day Co-Parenting Finance Action Plan

30 Days:

- Review your custody agreement
- List all recurring and upcoming shared expenses
- Choose a method of communication and documentation

60 Days:

- Propose a shared cost plan to your co-parent
- Test a system for reimbursements and recordkeeping
- Have a conversation (or send a message) to clarify expectations

90 Days:

- Evaluate what's working and what's not

- Adjust agreements as needed
- Celebrate your progress—even if it's just having one less argument

Final Reflection: Your Kids Deserve Peace—And So Do You

Co-parenting and finances will never be perfect. But they can be respectful. They can be manageable. And they can absolutely be healthy.

You are allowed to set boundaries. You are allowed to stop engaging in financial games. You are allowed to protect your child's needs—and your own nervous system.

This isn't just about receipts and reimbursements. It's about creating a life where your kids don't have to absorb the tension. Where you can model maturity, self-respect, and emotional safety.

You're not just raising children. You're raising future adults. Let your co-parenting finances reflect the kind of calm, structure, and grace you want your kids to carry forward.

And if no one's told you this yet: You're doing better than you think.

Chapter 24: Dating, Remarrying, and Money Conversations the Second Time Around

Love, Trust, and a Little Financial PTSD

Let's talk about something nobody really warns you about after divorce: falling in love again.

It's not just about dating apps, awkward dinners, or figuring out how to flirt after years in sweats. It's about trust. Emotional trust. Physical trust. *Financial* trust.

Because when you've been through the emotional, legal, and financial unraveling of a marriage, the idea of starting over—of sharing again—can feel just as scary as it does exciting.

You might be asking:

- "How do I talk about money without ruining the vibe?"
- "What if they have debt?"
- "What if I've finally gotten stable, and blending finances blows it all up again?"
- "How can I protect what I've rebuilt, without pushing love away?"

This chapter is here to help you walk into love the second time around with eyes wide open, heart cautiously hopeful, and financial wisdom in your back pocket.

This isn't about fear. It's about *freedom.* The freedom to choose again, *and* to protect what you've built in the process.

Section 1: Why Money Conversations Are Harder the Second Time

Let's be honest: divorce leaves scars. Even if it was amicable. Even if it was necessary. Even if you're "over it."

You remember the financial fights. The secrets. The power struggles. The credit card arguments. The silence around spending. The trust that broke when the numbers didn't add up.

So now, when someone asks "What's your five-year plan?" you might freeze. Or flinch. Or deflect with humor.

And yet, if you're going to open your heart again, you'll eventually need to open your financial books, too.

Emotional Hurdles to Address:

- Fear of being financially used or taken advantage of again
- Guilt about having "less" (or more) than a new partner
- Shame about past debt, spending, or financial mistakes
- Trauma around financial control or neglect in your previous marriage

And here's the good news: You can work through all of this. One conversation, one boundary, one decision at a time.

Section 2: Dating and Finances – How Soon Is Too Soon?

Let's start with early-stage dating. You don't need to bring up your credit score on the second date. But eventually, if the relationship shows potential, these conversations matter.

When to Talk About Money:

- **Before cohabitation**
- **Before sharing big purchases or vacations**
- **Before getting engaged**
- **Before combining finances**

The earlier you can normalize *talking* about money, the less awkward it will feel when you're making real decisions together.

Questions to Gently Introduce Financial Topics:

- "What's your philosophy around money—are you more of a saver or spender?"
- "How do you usually handle things like budgeting or paying bills?"
- "What was money like in your last relationship?"
- "What's your biggest financial goal right now?"

These aren't interrogations. They're invitations to connect—with honesty and curiosity.

Section 3: Financial Red Flags in a New Relationship

Love can make us ignore things we shouldn't. So let's look at red flags clearly, before the butterflies talk you out of your instincts.

Red Flags to Watch For:

- Refusal to talk about money or avoidance of the topic entirely
- Asking to borrow money early in the relationship
- Not being upfront about debt, income, or financial obligations
- Pressuring you to combine finances quickly
- Negative patterns with child support or spousal support (their own or

yours)

If you spot these, *pause*. Talk to someone you trust. Listen to your gut. Financial behavior is often a window into emotional maturity—and long-term compatibility.

Section 4: When It Gets Serious – What to Discuss Before Remarrying

So you've found someone special. It's real. It's grounded. It's hopeful. And now... it's serious.

Before you walk down the aisle (again), move in, or merge money, there are critical conversations you need to have—no matter how in love you are.

The Big Topics to Cover:

1. **Income** – How much each of you makes, and from where.
2. **Debt** – Credit cards, student loans, business loans, old tax bills—everything.
3. **Assets** – Homes, retirement accounts, investments, valuable personal property.
4. **Kids and Financial Support** – From previous marriages or current co-parenting arrangements.
5. **Retirement Plans** – How are you preparing for later-life income, individually or together?
6. **Credit History** – This affects any future shared financial decisions like buying a home or car.
7. **Spending Habits** – What's normal for each of you? Where are the differences?
8. **Financial Roles** – Who pays what? Who manages what? What's shared versus separate?

Pro Tip: Don't try to do all this in one conversation. Spread it out. Build safety. Keep it open and judgment-free.

Section 5: To Combine or Not to Combine – Structuring Finances in a Second Marriage

There's no one "right" way to manage money in a relationship. But after divorce, many people find that *keeping some things separate* brings peace of mind and practical clarity.

Common Models for Managing Money:

1. **All-In Approach**

- Combine all income and expenses
- Joint accounts for everything

Pros: Simplicity, transparency, shared purpose

Cons: Can feel risky if one person is less responsible or earns significantly less/more

2. **Yours, Mine, and Ours Approach**

- Each partner keeps their own account
- A shared account is used for joint bills, housing, and family costs
- Each contributes a percentage or dollar amount based on income

Pros: Maintains autonomy and clarity

Cons: Requires regular communication and coordination

3. **Completely Separate**

- No shared accounts
- Each person pays their share of expenses individually

Pros: Maximum independence

Cons: Can feel disconnected or like "roommates"

Action Step: Pick a system that reflects your values, lifestyle, and emotional needs. There is no wrong answer—only what works best for both of you.

Section 6: Protecting Yourself the Second Time Around – Legal and Financial Tools

You're wiser now. You've learned. And one of the smartest things you can do when entering a second marriage is *protecting your peace*—and your finances.

Consider These Tools:

- **Prenuptial Agreement**: This isn't unromantic—it's responsible. It sets expectations, outlines property and debt ownership, and protects what you've already built.
- **Postnuptial Agreement**: Can be created after marriage, especially if your situation changes (inheritance, children, new business).
- **Estate Planning Updates**: Wills, beneficiaries, powers of attorney—all should be updated before or shortly after remarrying.
- **Separate Property Declarations**: For assets you want to remain solely yours (like an inherited home or premarital retirement account).
- **Trusts for Children from a Previous Marriage**: Protects their inheritance, especially in blended families.

Pro Tip: Meet with a financial planner and estate attorney together *before* tying the knot. You'll walk in with clarity and walk out with confidence.

Section 7: Blending Families and Budgets

Love might bring your hearts together, but shared bills, kids, and financial obligations? That's where things get real.

When you or your new partner bring children into the relationship, the financial dynamics multiply—school expenses, co-parenting obligations, college planning, household contributions, and daily costs of raising a blended family.

What to Consider When Blending Financial Lives with Kids:

1. Who pays for what?

If both of you have kids from previous relationships, will you:

- Contribute equally to all kids?
- Keep "yours" and "mine" expenses separate?
- Split by percentage of income?

2. What happens during holidays, vacations, and birthdays?

Are you expected to match your ex's spending style? Your new spouse's? Set a family budget early and align on expectations.

3. Are child support or alimony payments part of the monthly household cash flow?

Be transparent about obligations. They impact your real financial picture—and your new partner deserves to understand that, just as you do.

4. Do you need a shared calendar for kid-related expenses?

Yes. Especially if multiple parents are involved. Documenting helps prevent future conflict.

5. Are you saving for college—together or separately?

Open 529 plans or custodial accounts early. Decide whether it's joint, proportional, or individually managed.

Blended Budgeting = Blended Communication

Don't assume your new spouse understands your parenting expenses. Don't assume they'll contribute the same way you do. Talk, document, and revisit often.

Section 8: Love After Loss – The Emotional Side of Financial Partnership

Money in a second relationship comes with emotional weight. You've both been hurt. You both know what it's like to share a life and see it fall apart.

That history can bring fear, hesitation, or overcorrection (like financial secrecy or over-controlling tendencies).

Here's how to create safety the second time around:

1. Acknowledge your past—but don't live there.

It's okay to say, "I get anxious around money because of how things went last time." That's honesty. That's growth.

2. Celebrate small financial wins together.

Did you pay off a credit card? Create a budget that works? Survive tax season with grace? That's a win—celebrate it.

3. Keep "money dates."

Once a month, sit down together. Review goals. Tweak the budget. Dream about your next vacation. Money doesn't have to be scary when you face it as a team.

4. Don't punish your new partner for your ex's financial behavior.

Trust has to be earned—but it also has to be given a chance.

Section 9: Real-Life Stories – Second Chances with Smarter Choices

Sophie, 46 – "We Kept It Separate, and That Saved Us"

Sophie had been through a nasty divorce that left her deep in debt. When she remarried, she and her new husband kept their accounts separate, but paid joint expenses through a shared household account. "It wasn't about distrust—it was about peace of mind. We check in monthly, and it works."

Maya, 39 – "The Prenup Was the Best Decision We Made"

Maya had inherited land from her parents and was worried about protecting it if things didn't work out. Her partner understood. They met with an attorney, drafted a prenup, and laid everything on the table. "It actually brought us closer. It gave me space to love him freely."

Terrance, 53 – "I Didn't Want to Merge My Pension. And That Was Okay."

Terrance had a government pension and didn't want to tie it to another marriage. He and his fiancée talked it through, agreed on a financial plan that respected his boundaries, and still built a future together. "We have a great relationship—and our own accounts."

Section 10: Remarrying and Retirement Planning

A second marriage changes the math on retirement—especially if you're marrying later in life or bringing different assets and timelines to the table.

Questions to Answer:

- Are you combining retirement savings?
- Will one person's Social Security affect the other's?
- Are you adjusting your investment strategy now that you're part of a couple?

- Do you plan to retire at the same time—or stagger your transitions?

Pro Tip: Run your retirement numbers together. Use a planner or online tools like SmartAsset or Fidelity's retirement score calculator to visualize your future.

Section 11: Estate Planning the Second Time Around

This is one of the most overlooked financial conversations in remarriage—and the most important.

Key Documents to Review:

- **Wills** – Does your new partner inherit everything? What about your kids?
- **Trusts** – Consider a revocable living trust to divide assets fairly and minimize court drama.
- **Beneficiary Forms** – Update retirement accounts, life insurance, bank accounts.
- **Healthcare Power of Attorney** – Who gets to make medical decisions if you're incapacitated?

Blended families can get messy if the paperwork isn't in place. Don't leave your loved ones confused, fighting, or legally tangled.

Section 12: 30/60/90-Day Financial Integration Plan

Here's a gentle roadmap for combining love and money intentionally.

Day 30:

- Share financial pasts (credit, debt, wins, mistakes)
- Compare spending styles and budgeting preferences
- Choose a co-budgeting app or system

Day 60:

- Create a shared household budget
- Discuss future goals (buying a home, vacations, saving)
- Decide on account structure (joint, separate, hybrid)

Day 90:

- Meet with a financial advisor together
- Begin estate planning updates
- Celebrate the clarity you've created

Final Reflection: Love Is Risky—But So Is Living Without It

Let's end with this: You're allowed to hope again.

You're allowed to fall in love and still have boundaries. You're allowed to want romance and a prenup. You're allowed to protect your peace while opening your heart.

This chapter wasn't about rules. It was about *options. Tools. Language.* It was about helping you build the confidence to walk into a second chance with wisdom—not walls.

You are not broken because your first marriage ended. You are experienced.

You are not foolish for loving again. You are brave.

And the love you build now—with shared values, mutual respect, and financial honesty—might just be the love that lasts.

Synopsis – Part 4: Long-Term Wealth and Confidence

P*art 4: Long-Term Wealth and Confidence* is the turning point in the journey from surviving divorce to thriving independently. This section is about reclaiming not just financial stability—but building wealth, legacy, and lasting peace of mind. Here, readers are invited to step into the role of long-term thinker, builder, and decision-maker. It's not about quick fixes or just "getting by"—it's about stepping into the future with clarity, confidence, and control.

This part walks readers through the complex yet empowering world of investing, career transitions, co-parenting financial systems, and forming new relationships without losing the progress they've made. It guides them on how to start investing with small amounts, pursue fulfilling work or education opportunities after time away, and navigate the emotional and financial complexities of dating or remarriage—especially when children, blended families, or differing money values are involved.

Readers will learn how to structure shared costs respectfully with ex-partners, blend finances with new partners wisely, and protect their peace while continuing to plan for retirement, estate, and generational wealth.

Throughout these chapters, the tone remains conversational, supportive, and rooted in real-life application. Each chapter offers tools, scripts, checklists, and reflections to help readers not only understand money—but trust themselves to manage it well.

The ultimate goal of Part 4 is not just financial security. It's about owning your worth, designing your future with intention, and knowing—without a doubt—that your best financial life is still ahead.

Chapter 25: Financial Goal Setting – For the Next 5, 10, and 20 Years

From "Just Getting By" to Living with Intention

You've walked through the fire. You've made it through sleepless nights, hard decisions, paperwork, quiet bank accounts, maybe even courtrooms and awkward handoffs at the kids' soccer games. Now, you're ready to look ahead.

This chapter isn't about survival. It's about strategy.

It's about planting financial seeds today that will grow into freedom, stability, and peace of mind in five years. Ten years. Twenty years.

It's about writing the next chapter of your life *on purpose.*

Financial goal setting after divorce isn't about rigid spreadsheets or fantasy timelines. It's about reclaiming your voice in the conversation about your own future. Even if that future looks different than what you once imagined.

We'll break this process down into three timelines:

- The next **5 years** – Your rebuilding phase
- The next **10 years** – Your expansion and stability phase
- The next **20 years** – Your legacy and long-term wealth phase

But first, we start where all goal setting should begin—not with numbers, but with *clarity.*

Section 1: The Foundation – Vision Before Numbers

Before we talk dollars, let's talk dreams.

Grab a notebook or open your notes app. Write this at the top:

"What do I want my life to look like in 5, 10, and 20 years?"

Don't filter it. Don't edit. Don't worry if it sounds unrealistic or emotional.

Just write.

Do you want to:

- Own a home?
- Pay off your student loans?
- Travel alone for the first time?
- Help your kids through college?
- Start a business?
- Retire without fear?
- Support your aging parents?
- Build generational wealth?

Your goals are yours. They don't have to be big. They just have to be *true.*

Once you've written them, you're ready to assign them a timeline—and a plan.

Section 2: The 5-Year Plan – Rebuild, Recalibrate, Restore

The first five years after a major life transition are about stabilization and rebuilding. This is where we get back on solid financial ground—and begin to move forward with confidence.

Your 5-Year Financial Goals May Include:

- Building (or rebuilding) an emergency fund
- Paying down debt
- Repairing your credit
- Securing stable housing
- Refinancing or consolidating loans
- Setting a savings target
- Starting (or restarting) retirement contributions
- Creating a post-divorce budget that reflects your *real* life

Let's Break It Down: How to Set Smart 5-Year Goals

1. **Be Specific**

- "Build emergency fund" → "Save $10,000 in emergency savings by December 2029."

1. **Make It Measurable**

- $10,000 ÷ 60 months = $167/month

1. **Make It Visual**

- Use a tracker on your fridge or inside your planner
- Watch your progress grow—motivation matters

1. **Automate Where You Can**

- Set up automatic transfers to savings
- Enroll in employer retirement plans or open a Roth IRA

1. **Stay Flexible, But Focused**

- If life throws you a curveball, adjust. Don't abandon.

Pros and Cons of 5-Year Planning:

Pros:

- Focuses your energy
- Creates achievable milestones
- Restores confidence quickly

Cons:

- Can feel overwhelming if goals are too big
- Easy to overplan without leaving margin for life's surprises

Tool Tip: Use a 5-Year Financial Timeline Spreadsheet with monthly check-ins. Include columns for:

- Goal
- Target amount
- Deadline
- Current progress
- Notes

Section 3: The 10-Year Plan – Growth, Stability, and Expansion

By the time you reach the ten-year mark, you're not just patching holes anymore. You're building something real. Something solid. Something sustainable.

The ten-year window is about growth—not just in your savings account, but in your mindset, your income, and your overall quality of life. It's where stability turns into opportunity.

Your 10-Year Financial Goals Might Include:

- Buying a home or upgrading from your current one
- Increasing retirement contributions to 15%+ of income
- Funding your child's education through a 529 plan or other savings vehicle
- Advancing your career or launching a side business
- Paying off remaining debts (student loans, car, credit cards)
- Establishing a fully funded emergency fund (6–12 months of expenses)
- Starting to invest outside of retirement accounts

This is your *build and breathe* phase. You're climbing out of survival mode and moving toward security—and choice.

How to Build Your 10-Year Goals (Without Burnout)

1. **Choose 3–5 Focus Areas** Don't spread yourself too thin. You don't need 20 goals—just the right ones.
2. **Create Tiered Goals** Break larger goals into mini-goals.

- "Save $60,000 for college" → "Save $500/month for 10 years."

1. **Use Percentages, Not Just Dollar Amounts**

- "Contribute 10% to retirement by year 5, increase to 15% by year 10."

1. **Plan for Real Life** Account for known life events:

- High school tuition
- Aging parents
- Health changes
- Housing transitions

1. **Revisit Annually** Goals shift as life does. Revisit your ten-year plan every 12 months and course-correct as needed.

Pros and Cons of 10-Year Planning:

Pros:

- Provides space to grow without pressure
- Keeps your eyes on the horizon
- Encourages discipline while allowing flexibility

Cons:

- Can feel distant or abstract
- Requires consistent motivation

Tool Tip: Use a 10-Year Vision Journal. Write letters to your future self. Track life goals alongside financial goals (travel, relationships, lifestyle shifts). Keep it soulful, not just statistical.

Section 4: The 20-Year Plan – Legacy, Longevity, and Long-Term Wealth

The twenty-year vision is not about fantasy. It's about *legacy*. It's about designing a future that reflects your deepest values and your highest hopes—for yourself, your children, and maybe even your community.

This is where wealth-building meets purpose. Where the seeds you've planted start to bloom into freedom, generosity, and peace of mind.

Your 20-Year Financial Goals Might Include:

- Reaching full retirement age with a fully funded retirement plan
- Paying off your mortgage
- Creating a giving plan or philanthropy goal
- Establishing a family trust
- Leaving an inheritance for children or grandchildren
- Becoming completely debt-free
- Writing a living will and full estate plan
- Moving into part-time work or passion-based work
- Fully funding college or vocational training for children

At this point, your money works *for* you, not the other way around.

How to Design Your 20-Year Wealth Plan

1. **Start With Your Legacy** Ask:

- What do I want to leave behind?
- Who do I want to impact?
- What does peace of mind look like in my later years?

1. **Calculate Your Retirement Number** Use online calculators or meet with a financial advisor to determine how much you'll need to retire securely. Consider:

- Healthcare costs
- Long-term care
- Housing transitions
- Travel and lifestyle goals

1. **Review Your Estate Plan** Ensure your:

- Will
- Trust (if applicable)
- Power of attorney
- Healthcare proxy
- Beneficiaries are all up to date and aligned with your values.

1. **Diversify Your Investments** By year 20, you should:

- Have multiple retirement accounts (401k, IRA, Roth IRA)
- Possibly own real estate
- Have diversified stock and bond holdings
- Understand your risk tolerance as you age

Pros and Cons of 20-Year Planning:

Pros:

- Helps you prepare for retirement with purpose
- Gives you long-term peace and perspective
- Encourages legacy-focused thinking

Cons:

- Easy to feel disconnected if retirement feels far away
- Requires regular education and adjustments

Tool Tip: Create a "Freedom Binder" with long-term goals, legacy letters to loved ones, and vision statements. Keep your financial documents, estate plans, and life goals all in one place.

Section 5: Turning Goals Into Systems – Because Willpower Isn't Enough

Setting a goal is one thing. Reaching it requires a *system*.

Willpower fades. Motivation wavers. But systems? They stick. They give you structure when life gets chaotic—and they help protect your progress when emotions or emergencies threaten to derail your plan.

The 5-Part Goal System

1. Automate

- Auto-transfer savings
- Auto-invest with apps or brokerages
- Auto-pay bills to avoid late fees

2. Visualize

- Use progress trackers, vision boards, or budgeting apps
- Watch your debt shrink or your savings grow

3. Check In Monthly

- 30-minute review of your money every month
- What went well? What needs to change?

4. Adjust Quarterly

- Every 90 days, zoom out. Are your goals still relevant?
- Life changes—so should your goals

5. Celebrate Small Wins

- Paid off a credit card? Saved your first $500? Celebrate it.
- Progress is powerful fuel

Remember: systems aren't rigid. They're *supportive.*

Section 6: Aligning Your Goals with Your Values

Financial goals mean nothing if they're not tied to something that matters.

It's not about hitting a number in your bank account—it's about what that number lets you *do*.

So ask yourself:

- Why do I want to be debt-free?
- What does financial peace mean to me?
- What kind of life am I building for myself... and my kids?
- What values do I want to teach my family through my money decisions?

Tie every goal to a deeper value. That's where the fire comes from.

Examples:

- "I want to save $50,000 for retirement" → "Because I never want my kids to feel burdened by my aging."
- "I want to buy a home" → "Because I want to create stability for my family that I never had growing up."
- "I want to get out of debt" → "Because I want to sleep at night and live with freedom."

Section 7: Real-Life Goal-Setting Stories

Monique, 45 – "I Started With $20 a Month"

After her divorce, Monique felt overwhelmed by retirement planning. She started saving just $20/month into a Roth IRA. "I couldn't believe how good it felt just to *start.* Now I'm up to $200/month, and it's second nature."

Darren, 52 – "We Made a 10-Year Plan Together"

Darren remarried after his kids were grown. He and his wife sat down and created a joint 10-year financial plan. "We review it every anniversary. It's actually brought us closer."

Janelle, 38 – "My Goal Wasn't Big—It Was Stability"

Janelle didn't care about early retirement. She wanted to stop living paycheck to paycheck. "I made one goal: to have three months of bills in savings. That changed my life."

Section 8: Financial Goal Pitfalls (And How to Avoid Them)

Pitfall #1: Setting Unrealistic Timelines

- "I'll pay off $30,000 in debt in one year!"
- *Instead*: Stretch the goal, but break it into manageable steps

Pitfall #2: Comparison Traps

- Don't compare your goals to someone else's Instagram highlight reel
- Focus on your starting point—not theirs

Pitfall #3: Abandoning Goals After One Slip

- One missed contribution doesn't mean you failed
- Adjust, realign, keep going

Pitfall #4: All or Nothing Thinking

- Saving $10 is better than saving nothing
- Progress > perfection

Section 9: Creating a Goal-Setting Ritual

Make goal setting a rhythm in your life, not a one-time event.

Sample Monthly Ritual:

- Light a candle. Pour coffee or tea.
- Review the past month's money progress
- Write 3 things that went well
- Write 1 thing you'll improve
- Update your savings or debt payoff tracker
- Revisit your 5, 10, and 20-year goals
- Speak one financial affirmation out loud:

> *"I am building the life I deserve, one decision at a time."*

Section 10: 5/10/20-Year Goal Planning Worksheets

Your 5-Year Goals

- What do you want to achieve by Year 5?
- Why does this matter to you?
- What systems will you put in place?

Your 10-Year Goals

- What would financial stability look like?
- What income, lifestyle, or assets do you want to have?
- What's your "stretch" goal that would excite you?

Your 20-Year Goals

- What legacy do you want to leave?
- How will your money reflect your values?
- What does retirement or semi-retirement look like for you?

Final Reflection: You're Not Just Setting Goals—You're Rewriting Your Future

You don't have to hit every goal perfectly.

You don't need to have all the answers.

You just need to *start*—with honesty, with courage, and with your eyes on a future that still belongs to you.

Let this chapter be your permission slip: to dream again. To plan again. To believe in your financial future not just as a possibility, but as a promise you're keeping to yourself.

You've rebuilt your foundation. Now it's time to raise the roof.

Chapter 26: Understanding Your Money Mindset After Divorce

The Voice in Your Head That Talks About Money

Let's begin with something most people don't talk about—because it's invisible:

Your *money mindset.*

That quiet voice in your head when you open your banking app.

That gut feeling when you swipe your card.

That deep breath before you open a bill.

That anxious thought when someone says, "Let's split it."

All of that is your money mindset talking. And after divorce? That voice often gets louder, heavier, more uncertain.

You may be asking:

- "Will I ever feel safe again with money?"
- "Why do I feel guilty spending, even on things I need?"
- "How come I panic every time I pay a bill?"
- "Why do I avoid looking at my bank account?"

That's what this chapter is about.

Because before we can build wealth or hit goals, we have to get *underneath* the numbers. We have to get to the root of how we *feel* about money—

especially after going through a financial and emotional rupture like divorce.

This isn't just about spreadsheets. This is about the stories you've been told, the patterns you've absorbed, and the beliefs you carry. The good news? You can change them. You can rewrite your money story from the inside out.

Let's go there—gently, honestly, and together.

Section 1: What Is a Money Mindset?

Your money mindset is the collection of beliefs, thoughts, emotions, and attitudes you hold about money. It shapes every financial decision you make—consciously or unconsciously.

It's not just about how much you earn or spend. It's about how you feel about:

- Earning
- Spending
- Saving
- Debt
- Investing
- Generosity
- Receiving

And the truth is, most of us never learned how to talk about—let alone *heal*—our money mindset.

Section 2: Where Your Money Mindset Comes From

You didn't invent your money beliefs in a vacuum. They were shaped by:

1. Childhood

- Did your parents argue about money?
- Were you told "we can't afford that" often?
- Did money feel scarce, stressful, or shameful?

2. Culture

- Did your community prize financial status?
- Were you taught to be frugal, generous, competitive, or secretive about money?

3. Religion

- Were you told it's more "spiritual" to be poor?
- Was wealth seen as a blessing—or a temptation?

4. Marriage

- Did your spouse control the money?
- Were you shamed for spending?
- Did you make more and feel guilty—or make less and feel powerless?

All of these experiences write scripts in your brain—scripts that often replay after divorce, especially when you're trying to stand on your own.

Section 3: Common Money Mindsets After Divorce

After a divorce, many people carry one or more of these emotional scripts when it comes to money:

1. The Scarcity Script

"There's never enough."

You feel like the money's going to run out—even if it's not. You hoard out of fear. You delay basic purchases. You panic over every unexpected cost.

2. The Guilt Script

"I shouldn't be spending on myself."

You feel bad for buying anything that isn't a bare necessity. You may feel especially guilty spending on joy—vacations, clothes, hobbies—because it feels selfish or indulgent.

3. The Avoidance Script

"If I don't look at it, it's not real."

You avoid opening statements, logging into accounts, or tracking your spending. You fear what you might find, so you stay in the dark.

4. The Shame Script

"I messed up. I'm bad with money."

You carry blame from the divorce, past debt, or bad decisions. You tell yourself you're just "not good with money," which keeps you from learning or trying.

5. The Overcompensation Script

"I'll make up for what they lost."

You overspend on your kids, take on too much, or ignore your budget because you feel responsible for making things feel "normal" again.

These aren't weaknesses. These are wounds. They deserve healing—not judgment.

Section 4: How Divorce Disrupts Your Financial Identity

Divorce doesn't just divide assets. It often fractures your *financial identity.*

You may have gone from:

- Dual income to single income
- Stay-at-home parent to job seeker
- Financially dependent to financially responsible
- Credit-shared to credit-rebuilding
- Shared goals to solo decision-making

That shift isn't just logistical. It's psychological.

You're not just paying new bills—you're redefining who you are with money.

So if it feels hard, overwhelming, or even terrifying... you're not alone. You're not failing. You're *adjusting.*

Section 5: Your New Money Story Begins Here

Let's rewrite the narrative.

Take a breath. Get still. And answer these questions—honestly.

1. What money beliefs did I inherit that no longer serve me?
2. What financial fears am I still carrying from my marriage?
3. What would "peace" with money feel like for me?
4. What's a money story I want to leave behind?
5. What's a new one I want to write?

You don't have to fix everything overnight. But you *can* shift how you think.

Section 6: Rebuilding a Healthy Money Mindset – Step by Step

Step 1: Create Safety With Money

- Build a small emergency fund (even $500 is a start)
- Auto-transfer a tiny amount into savings each week
- Use a budgeting app or printable that feels intuitive—not stressful

Step 2: Separate Emotion From Math

- "This bill is a number—not a verdict on my worth"
- "My bank balance is information—not identity"
- Practice saying: "This is just data."

Step 3: Use Gentle Language

Change your inner dialogue from:

- "I suck at money" → "I'm learning something new"
- "I'll never catch up" → "I'm making progress"
- "I can't afford anything" → "That's not in the plan right now, but I'm working on it"

Language matters. Talk to yourself like you would your best friend.

Section 7: Tools for Shifting Your Mindset

Healing your money mindset after divorce isn't just about knowing what to do—it's about practicing it consistently. Here are tools to support that emotional and mental shift:

1. Money Journal

Each week, write:

- One money win
- One money challenge
- One emotion you felt while handling money
- One thing you're proud of

This helps you notice patterns, reframe shame, and stay grounded in growth.

2. Money Affirmations

Affirmations are not fluff—they're pattern interrupters. Choose 1–3 to repeat daily:

- "I am rebuilding with wisdom and strength."
- "Every dollar I manage well builds my future."
- "I release shame and choose strategy."

Write them on sticky notes. Put them on your mirror, fridge, or phone screen.

3. Body Awareness

Your body knows when you're in financial fear. Your chest tightens. Your jaw clenches. Your breath shortens.

When you notice this happening:

- Pause
- Name it: "This is financial fear."
- Breathe: Inhale for 4, hold for 4, exhale for 6

- Return to the numbers when your nervous system has calmed

Money decisions made in fear often hurt more than help.

Section 8: Rewriting Your Identity – You Are the CFO of Your Life Now

It's easy to feel like someone else used to run the financial show—and now you've been thrown into the lead role without rehearsal.

But here's the truth: You *are* the CFO of your life now. And you are qualified. You are capable. You are learning. You are building the muscle.

Start acting like the CEO you already are:

- Set goals and track progress
- Review your "business" monthly (aka your personal budget)
- Take meetings with yourself—every 30 days, sit down and look at your numbers
- Ask for help when needed—advisors, coaches, books, apps

No business runs without review and support. You shouldn't be expected to either.

Section 9: Real-Life Mindset Shifts After Divorce

Danielle, 40 – "I Was Scared to Check My Account"

"I used to wait days to look at my balance, hoping nothing had overdrafted. After the divorce, I made a rule: I check it every Friday morning with my coffee. Now it's a habit—and I don't feel anxious anymore."

Rob, 51 – "I Thought Money Made Me a Failure"

"My ex made more, and I felt small. When we split, I realized I had a scarcity mindset from childhood. I started therapy, got a coach, and now I'm debt-free and saving for a condo. My mindset had to shift before the numbers could."

Trina, 37 – "I Let Myself Spend on Joy"

"I used to feel guilty buying anything fun. After divorce, I budgeted $40/month for joy. Coffee dates, thrift shop finds, a new book. It changed everything. I'm allowed to feel good about money again."

Section 10: When to Get Help With Money Mindset

You don't have to heal alone. If you're struggling with:

- Panic attacks related to money
- Avoidance so deep it's affecting your livelihood
- Beliefs that you're "unworthy" of wealth or stability
- Emotional flashbacks related to financial trauma

It's okay to seek help. A trauma-informed therapist, financial coach, or even a divorce recovery group can provide tools and community.

There is no shame in getting support. In fact, it's one of the strongest moves you can make.

Section 11: Your Mindset Reset Plan – 30, 60, 90 Days

Day 30:

- Start a money journal
- Choose and use 1 affirmation daily
- Set a weekly "money check-in" ritual (same time each week)

Day 60:

- Read a book or listen to a podcast about money mindset
- Write a "Dear Future Me" letter describing your new financial self
- Track all income and expenses for one month (just observe)

Day 90:

- Review your progress
- Identify one belief that has shifted
- Celebrate it with a small act of joy

This is healing. This is growth. This is you becoming someone who is at *peace* with money.

Final Reflection: You're Not Starting Over—You're Starting Real

You've been told a lot of things about money. Some helpful. Some harmful. Some that weren't even yours to carry.

But here you are. Still standing. Still building. Still trying.

That makes you powerful.

This chapter wasn't about budgets or debt payoff plans. It was about the stories in your mind—and your choice to write new ones.

You can walk into your financial future with love, logic, and leadership.

Because you're not just managing money now—you're managing *meaning*. And you're doing it with wisdom you earned the hard way.

Take a breath. Look at how far you've come. Then take the next step forward.

This is your new money story.

And it's going to be a good one.

Chapter 27: Financial Trauma and How to Heal From It

When Money Isn't Just Math—It's Pain

Let's be honest—sometimes, money hurts.

It's not just the credit score, the overdraft fees, the overdue notices. It's the weight. The shame. The helplessness. The fear that clings to you long after the account is closed or the debt is paid.

That's what financial trauma feels like.

And for so many people who've gone through divorce, it's not just about the dollars. It's about what those dollars represented: control, betrayal, silence, abandonment, chaos.

This chapter isn't just about budgeting or credit repair. It's about healing.

Healing from being financially ignored. Healing from being lied to about money. Healing from feeling like your worth was tied to your bank account. Healing from the moments when you felt powerless, unseen, or unsafe.

If money has ever made you cry, freeze, rage, or shut down—this chapter is for you.

Let's talk about it. Let's name it. And then, let's walk through the steps to release it.

Section 1: What Is Financial Trauma?

Financial trauma is the emotional and psychological response to a situation involving money that overwhelms your nervous system, damages your sense of safety, and leaves you feeling powerless or afraid.

It's trauma rooted not in physical harm, but in financial harm—or in the emotional fallout of financial stress, instability, or control.

It often stems from:

- Divorce or separation
- Financial abuse or manipulation by a partner
- Job loss or income instability
- Sudden poverty or bankruptcy
- Childhood neglect or generational poverty
- Medical debt or caregiving responsibilities
- Growing up in a home where money was chaotic, scarce, or secret

And it doesn't just disappear when the bills are paid.

Section 2: Signs You May Be Carrying Financial Trauma

You might not have called it trauma. You might have called it stress, overwhelm, anxiety, or just "how life is." But trauma has a way of showing up, even when we try to suppress it.

Here are some signs that financial trauma might still be affecting you:

- **Avoidance**: You can't bring yourself to open bills, check your bank account, or talk about money.
- **Overcontrol**: You obsess over every penny, fearing even the smallest expense will derail you.
- **Underspending**: You don't allow yourself to enjoy your money—even when you can afford to—because you're afraid it'll vanish.

- **Overspending**: You use spending to cope with anxiety, loneliness, or pain, then feel guilt and shame.
- **Panic Responses**: You feel physical anxiety (tight chest, short breath, stomach aches) when making financial decisions.
- **Freeze Mode**: You feel so overwhelmed by financial decisions that you shut down and make none at all.
- **Relational Triggers**: Money conversations with your ex, co-parent, or new partner cause disproportionate fear or defensiveness.
- **Shame Narratives**: You constantly think "I'm bad with money" or "I'll never get ahead."

If you see yourself in these, you're not broken. You're not dramatic. You're human—and your nervous system is responding to past pain.

The good news? That pain can be rewired. And it starts with awareness.

Section 3: Where Financial Trauma Comes From

Understanding the root of your trauma can help you loosen its grip.

1. From a Former Spouse or Partner

- They controlled the money and left you in the dark.
- They hid debt or drained accounts.
- They made you feel stupid or dependent.
- They punished you with money, using it to control where you could go, who you could see, or what you could buy.

2. From Your Upbringing

- You watched your parents fight about money.
- You were taught that money is evil, shameful, or not to be talked about.
- You never saw an example of financial security or healthy financial conversations.

- You were the "fixer" or "helper" in a financially unstable home.

3. From Crisis or Loss

- You went from financial safety to instability overnight.
- A health crisis or job loss wiped out your savings.
- You had to rebuild from scratch after leaving an unsafe situation.

Trauma doesn't always come from dramatic events. Sometimes, it's the slow drip of instability, anxiety, and neglect.

But no matter the source, your story deserves compassion—not judgment.

Section 4: The Science Behind It – Why Money Trauma Stays In Your Body

Financial trauma is real trauma. Your brain and body don't differentiate between financial stress and other types of threat.

When you've experienced financial trauma:

- Your brain becomes hyper-vigilant. You scan for danger—even when there's none.
- Your nervous system goes into fight, flight, freeze, or fawn mode around money.
- Your decision-making shuts down when you feel unsafe.
- Your emotions override logic, making simple financial tasks feel impossible.

It's not that you're irresponsible. It's that your body has learned that money = danger.

The path to healing is helping your body feel safe again—while you slowly rewrite the patterns in your brain.

Section 5: How to Begin Healing Financial Trauma

Healing is not about being perfect with money. It's about learning to feel *safe* with money. It's about replacing panic with presence, fear with facts, and shame with strategy.

Here's where we start.

Step 1: Acknowledge the Trauma Without Judgment

Say it out loud or write it down:

> *"Something happened that changed the way I feel about money."*

You don't need to justify it. You don't need to minimize it. Just honor it.

Trauma thrives in silence. Healing begins with naming the truth.

Step 2: Build Micro-Moments of Safety With Money

You don't need to overhaul everything overnight. Start by taking *tiny* steps.

- Open your bank app once a day, even just to glance.
- Check your balance and say out loud:

> *"This is information, not a threat."*

- Set a 10-minute timer to review one financial task—then stop.
- Reward yourself afterward. Make it feel safe. Make it feel kind.

Think of it like exposure therapy. You're gently showing your nervous system: "We can handle this."

Step 3: Separate the Past From the Present

Say this to yourself:

> *"That was then. This is now. I am in control now."*

Visualize yourself stepping out of the financial shadows of your past—whether that's a toxic relationship, an unstable household, or a time of fear.

Light a candle. Write a goodbye letter to the financial pain you've carried. Burn it safely. Breathe deeply.

Ceremony matters. It helps your body *know* you're moving forward.

Step 4: Learn the Skills You Weren't Taught

Many of us were handed fear—but never given tools.

Here's where education becomes medicine.

- Learn how credit works—not from fear, but from power.
- Understand how to build a simple budget that respects your life.
- Learn about saving, investing, insurance, and planning—not because you "should," but because it gives you choice.

Let learning be your protest against the chaos.

Step 5: Get Support

Healing financial trauma often requires support—just like any other type of trauma.

Consider:

- A therapist (especially trauma-informed or somatic)
- A financial coach who focuses on emotional wellness

- A support group for divorce, debt recovery, or financial independence
- Books, podcasts, or communities that normalize healing money stories

You don't have to do this alone. And you don't have to do it ashamed.

Section 6: Emotional Triggers and How to Manage Them

Financial trauma doesn't just live in your past. It shows up in the present—in everyday decisions, interactions, and reactions.

Here are common triggers and how to gently disarm them:

Trigger 1: An Unexpected Bill

Reaction: Panic, racing thoughts, shame spiral

Response: Pause. Breathe. Say out loud:

> *"This is stressful, but it's solvable. I can break this into steps."*
>
> *Create a plan: call the provider, negotiate, ask for a payment plan.*

Trigger 2: A Financial Conversation With Your Ex

Reaction: Defensive tone, emotional flooding, avoidance

Response: Set a boundary: "Let's keep this about the kids and the numbers."

Write your points down beforehand. Use text or email if voice calls escalate emotions. Document everything.

Trigger 3: Looking at Your Credit Score

Reaction: Shame, fear of being "judged" by a number

Response: Say to yourself:

"This number reflects a season—not my worth."

Create a 3-month plan to improve it—tiny changes count. Celebrate effort.

Trigger 4: Your Kids Asking for Something You Can't Afford

Reaction: Guilt, inadequacy, overcompensating

Response: Be honest:

> *"Right now, that's not in the budget. But let's put it on a wish list and talk about how we can work toward it."*
>
> *Teach them that money has boundaries—and that doesn't mean they're unloved.*

Section 7: Rebuilding Trust With Yourself

Financial trauma often creates one major wound: a loss of *self-trust.*

You might think:

- "I always mess this up."
- "I should've seen the signs."
- "I can't be trusted with money."

Let's call those lies what they are: echoes of trauma. Not truth.

Here's how to rebuild trust with yourself:

1. Keep Small Promises

Say, "I'll review my budget every Sunday"—and do it.

Say, "I'll transfer $10 to savings this week"—and do it.

Every time you follow through, you tell your brain:

> *"I can count on me."*

2. Forgive Your Past Self

Write a letter to the version of you that overspent, trusted the wrong person, ignored the red flags. End it with:

> *"You were doing the best you could. I forgive you. I've got us now."*

3. Track Wins, Not Just Goals

Every week, write down three money wins—no matter how small.

- "I checked my balance every day."
- "I said no to something that didn't fit my budget."
- "I asked for help."

Progress builds confidence. Repetition builds trust.

Section 8: Your Nervous System and Your Net Worth

Here's a truth that changed everything for many readers:

You cannot budget from a place of panic.

That's not you being "bad with money." That's your nervous system being hijacked.

When your brain perceives threat—real or emotional—it shuts down executive functioning (the part that plans, calculates, decides). It floods you with cortisol, fear, and a need to escape.

This is why you might:

- Freeze instead of paying bills
- Avoid money talks with your partner
- Spend impulsively just to feel relief

Tools to Regulate While Making Money Decisions:

- Breathe in for 4, hold for 4, exhale for 6. Repeat 5x.
- Use a weighted blanket while reviewing your finances
- Put on calming music or nature sounds
- Sip something warm while you budget
- Set a 15-minute timer—then stop

Your brain needs to *feel safe* in order to think clearly. Protect your peace before you protect your portfolio.

Section 9: Building a New Relationship With Money

Healing financial trauma isn't just about avoiding pain—it's about creating *joy* and *trust* with money again. You deserve a relationship with money that feels:

- Calm
- Empowered
- Intentional
- Honest
- Secure

Here's how to start building it.

Step 1: Define What "Healthy Money" Means to You

What does a peaceful relationship with money *look* like?
For some, it's:

- Paying bills without panic
- Saving without scarcity

- Spending without shame
- Talking about money with openness

Write your definition down. Read it weekly. Let it become your new blueprint.

Step 2: Anchor Your Financial Practices in Ritual

When money tasks feel like rituals, not chores, your body and mind begin to associate them with *safety* and *structure.*

Examples:

- "Money Mondays": review your spending, bills, and savings over coffee
- "Freedom Fridays": transfer to savings and reflect on progress
- "Debt-Free Dinners": every month, cook a meal that's aligned with your money values

Turn routines into rituals. Make peace a practice.

Step 3: Reclaim Joy Around Money

You are allowed to feel *good* with money. Even if you're not "there yet." Even if you're still healing.

- Create a "Joy Budget" line for monthly guilt-free spending
- Start a "Dream Fund" for something that lights you up
- Tip someone generously when it feels right
- Give yourself permission to enjoy a luxury within your means

Joy is not the opposite of responsibility. It's part of the healing.

Section 10: 30/60/90 Day Financial Trauma Healing Plan

This isn't a sprint—it's a re-entry. A rewiring. Here's how to start.

Day 30:

- Begin a money journal (3 minutes a day)
- Choose one financial task each week (balance check, pay a bill)
- Repeat this daily:

> *"Money is no longer my enemy. I am learning to feel safe with it."*

Day 60:

- Read one book or listen to a podcast about healing financial trauma
- Set a weekly "money ritual" time and protect it
- Track your financial wins (not just numbers—behaviors, too)

Day 90:

- Reflect on what's changed in your emotions and habits
- Meet with a therapist, coach, or accountability partner
- Celebrate the fact that you showed up—for yourself, for your healing

Final Reflection: From Pain to Power

Financial trauma is heavy. But it is not permanent.

It may have shaped your past. It may still whisper when you try something new. But it does *not* get to define your future.

You get to define your future.

You get to decide what safety looks like. What stability feels like. What wealth means to *you*.

And you don't have to do it all at once.

You just need to take the next right step. With gentleness. With grace. With the belief that financial healing isn't just possible—it's already unfolding.

This isn't about becoming someone new.

It's about becoming more fully, freely, powerfully *you*.

You've carried enough weight.

Now, it's time to build something beautiful.

Chapter 28: Teaching Your Kids About Money After a Divorce

The Most Important Lessons Aren't Taught—They're Lived

Let's get one thing straight right from the beginning:

You don't have to be perfect with money to raise financially smart kids.

You just have to be *present* with money. Honest about it. Intentional with it.

Your kids are watching. They're absorbing. And what they need most right now isn't a financial seminar—it's *you.*

They need to see what rebuilding looks like. They need to hear what financial boundaries sound like. They need to feel what security—even in transition—can still offer.

After divorce, your relationship with money is changing. But so is theirs. They're feeling the shifts. They're noticing what's different. And if you don't guide the narrative, someone—or something—else will.

That's why this chapter is so important.

This isn't just about allowances and savings jars (though we'll get there). It's about emotional literacy. Financial confidence. And showing your kids that even in the middle of a hard chapter, you can still write a better ending.

Section 1: Why Teaching Kids About Money After Divorce Hits Different

When you're co-parenting, budgeting on one income, or still finding your financial footing, talking to your kids about money can feel… loaded.

You might be thinking:

- "I don't want to scare them."
- "I don't want them to feel like they're a burden."
- "I don't want them to know how hard this is."

But here's what's also true:

- Silence creates confusion.
- Shame creates secrecy.
- Avoidance creates anxiety.

What your kids need is not every detail—they need *truth with tenderness.*

> *"Things are different now, but we're going to be okay." "We're being more thoughtful about how we spend, because that's how we build a better future." "You don't need to worry about the grown-up stuff, but I want to teach you how money works so you feel strong and smart."*

Section 2: What Your Kids Actually Need to Learn About Money—Now

Kids don't need a full financial curriculum to grow up financially literate. What they *do* need is consistent exposure to core money concepts in a way they can understand, connect with, and eventually practice.

Here's what to focus on, age by age.

For Younger Kids (Ages 4–10)

- **Money is a tool, not a toy** – Help them see that money helps us trade for things we need and value.
- **Saving feels good** – Let them experience the reward of waiting and watching money grow.
- **Choices matter** – Introduce the idea that money decisions mean trade-offs.

Simple Actions:

- Use a clear jar for saving so they *see* money accumulate.
- Let them "pay" for something small at the register with your supervision.
- Play "grocery store" or "bank" games to teach the flow of money.

For Tweens (Ages 11–13)

- **Budgeting basics** – Introduce the idea of income vs. expenses.
- **Wants vs. needs** – Reinforce the difference and talk about family priorities.
- **Earning matters** – Talk about how you earn money and how they can too.

Simple Actions:

- Give a modest allowance tied to responsibilities.
- Teach them how to split money into "save, spend, give" categories.
- Review a real receipt together and talk about what was worth it.

For Teens (Ages 14–18)

- **Banking and budgeting** – Show them how to use a checking account, savings account, and budget app.
- **Credit and debt** – Explain how credit works and why debt can be dangerous.
- **Income and taxes** – Help them understand paychecks, withholdings, and first jobs.

Simple Actions:

- Set them up with a teen checking account or prepaid debit card.
- Review your monthly budget (at a high level) and let them ask questions.
- Share your real-life mistakes and lessons with honesty and humility.

Section 3: Talking About Money Without Transferring Fear

Let's pause here for something important:

You can be honest without being heavy.

Your kids don't need the weight of your financial stress. But they do need your leadership.

Here's how to balance both:

Instead of

> *"We're broke. You can't have anything right now."*
>
> ***Try***
>
> *"This month, we're focusing on needs and saving for some bigger wants later. Let's talk about what matters most to you."*

Instead of

> *"I can't buy you what your dad/mom does."*
>
> ***Try***

"Different homes have different rules and budgets. In this house, we make thoughtful choices so we can take care of what matters."

Instead of

"You don't need to know about money—you're a kid."

Try

"I want to teach you a little more about how money works so you grow up feeling strong and capable."

You're not robbing your kids of childhood by talking about money. You're *equipping them for adulthood*—one real conversation at a time.

Section 4: How to Model Healthy Money Behaviors After Divorce

Kids don't just listen—they *watch.* Your behavior with money teaches more than your words ever could.

So how do you model financial health when you're still in recovery mode?

You show the process. You show the effort. You show the *intentionality.*

Here's how:

1. Let Them See You Budget

Even if it's simple. Even if it's messy.

"I'm sitting down to plan the week's money—want to help me guess the grocery total?"

Let them see that budgeting isn't about restriction—it's about awareness and power.

2. Talk About Choices

> *"We're skipping takeout this week because we're saving for the trip to grandma's." "I'm comparing prices because I want to get the best value."*

Every choice you explain becomes a teaching moment.

3. Celebrate Wins Together

> *"I paid off another credit card!" "We hit our emergency savings goal!"*

Let them see your pride. Let them feel your progress. They'll absorb your sense of empowerment.

4. Own Your Mistakes Without Shame

> *"I overspent this month, and I had to adjust. I learned something."*

This teaches resilience, not fear. It also shows them that mistakes are part of growth.

5. Stay Consistent With Your Money Rules

Whether it's about allowance, shopping, or birthday budgets—consistency builds safety. If things are tight, explain the "why," not just the "no."

Consistency says: "You can trust me to tell you the truth and to stick to what I say."

Section 5: Dealing With Co-Parenting Money Differences

Now let's talk about one of the hardest parts: what to do when you and your co-parent don't align on money.

You may be frugal—they're flashy.

You budget tightly—they spend freely.

You teach saving—they reward with gifts.

This can create confusion, resentment, and tension—not just for you, but for your kids.

What You Can Control:

- **Your household values**
- **Your tone and transparency**
- **Your consistency**

Let them know:

> *"In this house, we save before we spend. That's how we show responsibility."*
>
> *"Different homes do things differently. That's okay. We do what feels right here."*
>
> *"You're not wrong for liking nice things—but let's talk about how we can plan for them."*

Avoid comparing or criticizing the other parent. It's tempting, but it only places your child in the middle. Model your values, not your frustrations.

Chapter 29: Giving Without Overextending – Helping Others Without Hurting Your Plan

The Giver's Dilemma: When Your Heart Says "Yes" but Your Wallet Whispers "No"

Let's start with the truth a lot of people are afraid to say:

You want to help.

You want to be there.

You want to give.

To your kids.

To your aging parents.

To your siblings, friends, church, or community.

To anyone who's hurting—because you know what that feels like.

But there's this voice. Quiet, but steady.

"What about me?"

"What about my rent?"

"What about my future?"

"What if I give too much and I fall behind again?"

That voice isn't selfish. That voice is sacred.

It's the part of you trying to make sure you don't break yourself to fix someone else.

This chapter is about honoring both your compassion *and* your capacity.

Because giving is good. But giving sustainably? That's wisdom. That's power. That's love that lasts.

Let's walk through how to do it—with grace, with boundaries, and with a plan.

Section 1: Why Giving After Divorce Feels So Complex

After divorce, your entire emotional and financial world shifts. You might be:

- Trying to re-establish independence
- Carrying guilt over what your kids "lost"
- Supporting your parents as they age
- Fielding calls from family who think you're still the "fixer"
- Struggling to say no without feeling like the bad guy

And layered into all of that is the pressure to prove:

> *"I've got it together."*
> *"I can still provide."*
> *"I'm still generous, even if I have less."*

But generosity isn't about martyrdom. It's about alignment.

> *Giving from a place of wholeness, not depletion.*
> *Giving from overflow, not obligation.*
> *Giving from wisdom, not worry.*

Section 2: The Emotional Roots of Overgiving

Before we jump into the practical steps, let's name the *emotional* reasons giving can become overwhelming—especially after a major life event like divorce.

1. Guilt

You may feel guilt about what your kids, your parents, or your community lost when your life changed. So you try to "make up for it" with money.

> *"They didn't ask for this."*
> *"I want to soften the blow."*
> *"I don't want them to suffer because of my choices."*

Guilt-driven giving is understandable—but it's not sustainable.

2. Shame

Sometimes we give because we're trying to prove we're okay.

> *"Look—I'm still generous!"*
> *"I didn't fall apart."*
> *"I'm not selfish like my ex accused me of being."*

Shame-driven giving isn't really about them—it's about trying to heal a wound inside you.

3. Fear

You might give because you're afraid of losing love, respect, or connection.

> *"If I don't help, they'll think I don't care."*

"What if they stop calling me?"
"What if I'm alone?"

Fear-based giving often sacrifices your security to protect someone else's feelings.

4. Legacy Pressure

If you grew up in a home where helping others was core to your identity, you may feel like saying no dishonors your past.

"This is what we do in this family."
"My parents gave even when we had nothing."
"I want to be remembered as someone who always showed up."

Legacy giving is beautiful. But it still needs boundaries.

Section 3: The Cost of Giving Without Boundaries

Let's get honest about what happens when giving goes unchecked.

Emotional Costs:

- Resentment
- Burnout
- Anxiety
- Guilt layered on top of exhaustion

Financial Costs:

- Dipping into emergency savings
- Delaying your own debt payoff
- Undermining your retirement plan

- Falling behind on bills

Overgiving may feel noble, but if it wrecks your financial future, it doesn't serve anyone—not even the person you're trying to help.

Real Talk Reminder:

> *"If helping them breaks you, it's not help—it's harm, just hidden in kindness."*

You are allowed to love people and still say no.
You are allowed to care deeply and still keep your budget.
You are allowed to support others without sacrificing yourself.

Chapter 30: Planning Your Legacy – Estate Planning as a Single or Remarried Individual

Legacy Isn't Just About What You Leave—It's About What You Intend

Let's talk about something many people avoid until it's too late: estate planning.

Now, I know—just reading the phrase might make your stomach drop a little.

You've already been through the emotional wringer.

You've already faced paperwork, lawyers, division, loss.

You've already questioned what's fair, what's kind, what's right.

But estate planning isn't about expecting the worst. It's about choosing what's best—*on your terms.*

It's not just for the ultra-wealthy. It's not just for the elderly. It's not just about who gets what when you're gone.

It's about peace of mind now.

It's about protecting your kids.

It's about honoring your wishes.

It's about living with intention, not just dying with a plan.

Whether you're staying single or building a new blended family, this chapter will guide you through what you need to know, what you need to do, and how to do it without losing your sanity.

This isn't about fear. It's about *freedom.*

Section 1: Why Estate Planning Is Especially Important After Divorce

Here's a truth most people don't hear until it's too late: divorce doesn't automatically update your estate plan.

If you haven't changed your will, your ex could still be listed as:

- Your healthcare proxy
- Your financial power of attorney
- The beneficiary of your life insurance
- The inheritor of your assets or home

If you've remarried and haven't updated your documents, things get even more complicated—especially if there are kids from multiple relationships.

And if you're single, you might assume "it'll just go to my kids." But that's not always automatic, either—especially if minors are involved or there's no legal plan in place.

An updated estate plan is how you say, with certainty:

> *"This is who I trust. This is who I protect. This is how I want things handled."*

And that? That's a powerful gift—to your loved ones and to yourself.

Section 2: What Estate Planning Really Is (and Isn't)

Let's start by demystifying the term. Estate planning isn't some exclusive club reserved for people with mansions and multi-million dollar portfolios.

Estate planning is simply the process of deciding:

- Who gets what you own
- Who handles your affairs if you're unable to
- Who makes decisions if you can't speak for yourself
- How to protect your loved ones—especially children

It includes things like:

- A will
- A living will (advance healthcare directive)
- Power of attorney (for finances and medical decisions)
- Beneficiary designations
- Trusts (in some cases)
- Guardianship nominations (if you have minor kids)

It's not:

- Just a one-time event
- Only for the elderly
- Something to wait on "until you have more money"

If you have people you care about—or anything you care about—estate planning is for you.

Section 3: Key Documents You Need to Update (Post-Divorce or Post-Remarriage)

Here's a checklist to walk through, no matter where you are in your post-divorce journey.

1. Your Will

This legal document outlines who receives your assets and who manages your estate.

- Revoke or update your old will immediately after divorce.
- Choose a new executor—someone you trust to carry out your wishes.
- List your current children, partner (if remarried), and other beneficiaries clearly.
- Include personal property (cars, jewelry, family heirlooms).

Pro Tip: A will *does not* override beneficiary designations on retirement accounts or insurance—those must be updated separately.

2. Your Beneficiary Designations

Go through every account you have and make sure the right people are listed.

Check your:

- Life insurance policies
- Retirement accounts (401(k), IRA, Roth IRA)
- Pensions
- Bank accounts with payable-on-death instructions

Common mistake: Leaving an ex listed by default because you never got around to changing it.

3. Power of Attorney (POA)

This document gives someone the legal authority to act on your behalf in financial matters if you're incapacitated.

Choose someone:

- You trust deeply
- Who understands your financial values
- Who won't be overwhelmed by paperwork or pressure

4. Healthcare Power of Attorney / Advance Directive

This gives someone authority to make medical decisions if you're unable to communicate.

Ask yourself:

- Who do I trust with my health choices?
- Would this person honor my values?

If you've remarried, be clear about who has this role, especially if your children are adults and might otherwise assume that responsibility.

Chapter 31: Building Wealth with Intention – Not Just Recovery, But Expansion

You Didn't Come This Far Just to Get Back to Zero

Let's pause for a second and honor what you've done.

You've rebuilt a budget.

You've faced your fears.

You've protected your kids.

You've sat across from hard conversations, lawyers, maybe even your own reflection—and kept going.

But now, something bigger is waiting.

This chapter is about moving beyond recovery. Beyond "getting back to where you were."

It's about stepping into *expansion.*

> *Not just surviving.*
>
> *Not just catching up.*
>
> *But growing something real. Something powerful. Something that's yours.*

Because wealth isn't just about money. It's about options. Access. Confidence. Freedom. Safety. Legacy.

This chapter isn't about perfection. It's about planting the right seeds—with intention.

Let's get clear, get strategic, and start building—on purpose.

Section 1: Why Post-Divorce Wealth Building Is Different

When you're coming out of divorce, you're not starting at square one. You're starting at square *real.*

You know what it feels like to lose. To stretch a dollar.

To be afraid of the future.

To watch a plan unravel.

But that experience gives you something powerful: *discernment.*

You don't chase flashy anymore—you crave stability.

You're not looking to impress—you're looking to protect.

You've already had chaos—now you want peace.

Post-divorce wealth building isn't fueled by ego. It's fueled by *clarity.*

You're not just earning to earn. You're building to *be free.*

Section 2: Define What Wealth Means to You

Before we talk investments, assets, or income strategies—we have to start with your definition.

Because if you don't define wealth, someone else will.

So grab a notebook and finish this sentence:

"To me, wealth means ___________________________."

Is it:

- Never worrying about a bill again?
- Retiring early to travel with your grandkids?
- Paying cash for your child's college?
- Having a fully stocked emergency fund?

- Buying back your time with flexibility?

Wealth is personal. If it's not aligned with your values, it won't stick.

Section 3: The Foundations of Intentional Wealth

Wealth isn't just about what you have—it's about how you *handle* what you have. Let's start with the cornerstones of building wealth after divorce, layer by layer.

1. Stability Before Scaling

You can't expand if you're still patching holes. Start here:

- A 3–6 month emergency fund
- A reliable, diversified income stream
- A working budget that reflects your *real* lifestyle
- Updated insurance coverage (life, health, disability)
- Debt plan (including payoff or restructuring strategy)

This isn't glamorous—but it's what wealth is built *on*.

2. Cash Flow Clarity

You need to know:

- What's coming in
- What's going out
- What's left to build with

Use tools like:

- **YNAB (You Need a Budget)**
- **EveryDollar**
- **Spreadsheets with monthly review times**
- Or a simple notebook and a Sunday ritual

Wealth requires *attention.* Not obsession. Just consistency.

3. Debt With Intention

Not all debt is bad—but all debt needs a plan.

Break it down:

- **Bad debt**: High-interest credit cards, payday loans
- **Gray area debt**: Car loans, personal loans
- **Strategic debt**: Mortgages, education with ROI, business loans

Use the **Avalanche Method** (highest interest first) or **Snowball Method** (smallest balance first). Or a hybrid. Just move. Consistently.

Debt doesn't disqualify you from wealth. But ignoring it will delay your growth.

Section 4: Investment Basics for Expansion

Now that the foundation is set, let's talk *multiplication.*

Investing isn't about gambling—it's about ownership.

Here's what to focus on:

Step 1: Know the Buckets

Your money can live in different "buckets":

- **Tax-deferred** (Traditional IRA, 401(k))
- **Tax-free** (Roth IRA, Roth 401(k))

- **Taxable** (Brokerage accounts)

Diversification isn't just about *what* you invest in—it's also about *where* you invest.

Step 2: Use Simple, Long-Term Vehicles

You don't need to pick stocks or time the market.
Try:

- Index funds (S&P 500, Total Market)
- Target-date retirement funds
- ETFs with low expense ratios

If you want to learn more, great. But you can build wealth with "boring" basics. Boring works.

Step 3: Automate Everything You Can

Set it. Forget it. Let it grow.

- Auto-transfer to Roth IRA each month
- Enroll in your 401(k)—and increase contributions annually
- Round-up apps (like Acorns) for micro-investing

Let time and compound interest do the heavy lifting.

Step 4: Rebalance Annually

Once a year, revisit your portfolio. Are you still aligned with your:

- Risk tolerance?
- Time horizon?

- Goals?

If not—adjust. This is where a financial advisor can help (even just once a year).

Part 5: Real Talk, Red Flags, and Recovery Tips

Part 5: *Real Talk, Red Flags, and Recovery Tips* is the final chapter stretch of your healing and rebuilding journey. It brings everything full circle by focusing on what most financial guides avoid—how to *actually* stay steady, empowered, and protected in real-life situations after divorce.

This section isn't just about financial tools. It's about pattern recognition. Boundary setting. Emotional resilience. You'll find honest, unfiltered guidance on navigating the hard conversations, recognizing red flags in new relationships (and within yourself), and learning how to give, rebuild, and grow without losing your progress.

Readers are walked through how to balance generosity with self-protection (*Giving Without Overextending*), what financial freedom truly feels like after choosing themselves (*The Power of Financial Independence*), and how to secure what matters most with proper documentation and intention (*Planning Your Legacy*).

It closes with a powerful chapter on shifting from mere survival to expansion—*Building Wealth with Intention*. This is where your healing turns into legacy. Where your plan meets your purpose.

Every chapter offers:

- Practical action steps
- Compassionate, real-world advice

- Tools for navigating both numbers *and* emotions

This part of the book helps readers stop bracing for the next hit—and start building for the next breakthrough. It's about owning your journey with clarity, courage, and compassion, all the way to the finish line—and beyond.

Chapter 32: Don't Fall for the Rebound – Emotional Spending and Financial Scams

Healing Doesn't Have to Come With a Price Tag

You've done a lot of heavy lifting.

You've survived the breakup, the paperwork, the awkward calls, the lonely holidays.

You've faced your budget, built new routines, and maybe even started to smile again.

And then—out of nowhere—you find yourself clicking "Buy Now" on a cart full of stuff you don't really need.

Or wiring money to someone who "really gets you."

Or signing up for something that feels a little… off… but you just want to feel better. Seen. Wanted.

That's what we're here to talk about.

Because sometimes, the most expensive part of divorce isn't legal fees or asset division—it's what comes after. The urge to *feel better fast.* The need to reclaim joy, confidence, or connection—by swiping, clicking, or trusting someone a little too soon.

This chapter isn't here to shame you. It's here to *protect* you. To help you slow down, think twice, and step away from the financial cliff's edge before it turns into regret.

Because healing should feel like freedom—not another bill.

And love, connection, and peace? You shouldn't have to pay extra for those.

Let's walk through what emotional spending and scams really look like, how to recognize them, and how to bounce back if you've already been there.

Section 1: What Emotional Spending Really Is (And Why It's So Common After Divorce)

Emotional spending is when you spend money to meet an *emotional* need instead of a financial one.

It sounds like:

- "I deserve this."
- "I've been through so much."
- "It's just one thing to make me feel better."
- "I'm tired of saying no to myself."
- "I need to start fresh—with everything."

And here's the thing—it's totally human. You're not broken. You're *responding to pain with comfort.*

But when comfort becomes costly? That's when we have to pause.

Section 2: Why You're Vulnerable to Emotional Spending Right Now

Let's be real: divorce cracks things wide open.

Your routines change. Your environment shifts. Your self-image takes a hit.

And in the midst of rebuilding everything, your brain—and your heart—are constantly seeking safety.

Enter spending.

Emotional spending becomes a quick hit of:

- Control ("I get to choose this")
- Pleasure ("This feels good")
- Identity repair ("This makes me feel like myself again")
- Escape ("At least I'm not thinking about the breakup for a second")

The problem isn't the spending itself—it's when it *replaces* real healing or starts to:

- Undermine your goals
- Create debt
- Trigger shame cycles
- Delay progress

If you've said, "I'll start saving once I feel better," or "I'm not even looking at my account this month," it's a sign that emotions are driving the bus.

And it's okay. It's also reversible.

Section 3: The Rebound Trap – Financial Decisions That Feel Like Love

Post-divorce, there's another type of spending trap: the rebound.

Not just romantic rebounds (we'll get there), but *life rebounds*—where you try to fix emotional pain with financial decisions.

Some common "rebound" moves include:

- Buying a new car (that stretches your budget)
- Booking a luxury vacation you haven't saved for
- Redecorating or refurnishing the whole house
- Joining a pricey program that promises "healing" or "empowerment"
- Signing up for high-fee coaching packages without vetting the person

These things *aren't bad in themselves*. But when they're driven by emotion, not strategy—they can create long-term setbacks.

Questions to Ask Before Any Big Purchase:

- "Would I still want this in 6 months?"
- "Is this a need, a want, or an emotional salve?"
- "Does this fit my long-term financial goals?"
- "Am I trying to impress, escape, or heal with this?"
- "Can I comfortably afford this—or am I hoping to 'figure it out later'?"

Give yourself a 72-hour pause rule on all major purchases. Time is clarity's best friend.

Section 4: Scams That Target the Divorced and Vulnerable

Now let's talk about something darker—but just as real: scams.

You're not just more likely to overspend post-divorce. You're also more likely to be *targeted*.

Here are the most common scams that prey on newly single or recently divorced individuals:

1. **Romance Scams**

These often start online. A charming, attentive person slowly builds trust... and eventually asks for money. They may say:

- They're stranded
- They need help with a business deal
- They'll pay you back
- They love you—but just need a little support

Warning signs:

- They avoid video chats or in-person meetings
- They move fast emotionally
- They ask for secrecy
- They want money wired, gift cards, or crypto

2. **Fake Investment or Business Opportunity Scams**

These scams often show up as:

- A "can't-miss" business opportunity
- Promises of quick returns with no risk
- Someone convincing you to cash out your retirement or refinance your home to "invest"

After divorce, when you're looking to rebuild fast or prove your financial savvy, these offers can sound tempting.

Red flags to watch for:

- Pressure to act fast ("This opportunity won't last!")
- Complicated jargon with no clear explanation
- Lack of transparency about where your money goes
- Unregistered or unlicensed companies

Remember: If it sounds too good to be true—it *is*.

3. **Legal or Document Scams**

Scammers may pose as:

- "Debt relief specialists"
- "Divorce recovery experts"
- Fake attorneys offering to "clean up your financial life"

They might ask for an upfront fee to:

- Settle debts
- Modify alimony or support orders
- Get you "free money" from a fake grant or lawsuit

Protect yourself:

- Verify credentials (use state bar directories, BBB, FINRA)
- Never share your Social Security number, banking info, or ID with someone who cold-calls or emails you
- Don't pay fees upfront for something that sounds too simple or too fast

Section 5: Real Talk—Why Smart People Still Get Caught

If you've fallen into emotional spending or been scammed, let's clear this up:

You are not dumb. You are not careless. You are not hopeless.

You were *hurting*. You were *rebuilding*. You were trying to find comfort, connection, or confidence.

Smart people get caught when they're tired, isolated, overwhelmed, or freshly wounded. That doesn't make you a fool. That makes you *human.*

What matters now is what you do next.

Section 6: How to Rebuild After an Emotional Financial Mistake

If you've overspent, gotten scammed, or made a financial rebound decision you regret—here's how to reset:

Step 1: Forgive Yourself

Say this:

> *"I made a decision with the tools and emotions I had at the time. I learned something. I forgive myself."*

Guilt and shame are *not* productive currencies. Release them.

Step 2: Assess the Damage

- Look at the total: How much was spent or lost?
- Are there recurring charges or payments still happening?
- Can you dispute anything (credit card, PayPal, bank fraud)?

Face the facts without spiraling. Data helps you plan.

Step 3: Create a Repair Plan

- If it's debt, use the snowball or avalanche method.
- If it's a scam, report it to:
- The **FTC** (reportfraud.ftc.gov)
- Your bank or credit card company
- Local authorities if money was stolen
- If it's emotional overspending, set a "**money cooldown**" rule:

No large purchases without a 3-day pause and accountability check.

Step 4: Rebuild Trust—Slowly

- Start with small, intentional wins
- Create a financial calendar (review every Sunday or first of the month)
- Celebrate sticking to your budget—even for a week

Wealth isn't built in giant leaps. It's built in *daily alignment.*

Chapter 33: Social Media, Comparison Traps, and Financial Peer Pressure

You Can't Build a Budget With Someone Else's Highlights

Let's get right to it: Social media can mess with your money mindset.

You log in just to scroll for a second, and suddenly it feels like *everyone* has it more together than you do.

- Your coworker just bought a house.
- Your cousin is on their third vacation this year.
- Your ex's new partner just posted about "spoiling their queen."
- Someone you barely know is now a financial coach, crypto millionaire, and traveling the world in luxury sweats.

And there you are...

Trying to get your grocery bill down.

Trying to cover child support and still save.

Trying to emotionally stabilize, let alone financially thrive.

That pressure? That quiet voice that whispers "You should be doing more"? That's not truth—it's a trap.

This chapter is about escaping that trap.

It's about reclaiming *your* pace, *your* plan, and *your* power.

Because your worth isn't measured in likes, and your success isn't defined by a filtered post.

Let's talk about the emotional weight of comparison, the reality behind the social media curtain, and how to build a financial life that feels *real*—not performative.

Section 1: Why Comparison Hits Harder After Divorce

Divorce reshapes your life in a thousand ways, and comparison sneaks in through every crack.

- You're rebuilding while others seem to be relaxing.
- You're starting over while your ex seems to be accelerating.
- You're healing, and it feels like everyone else already got the happy ending.

Why does this sting so much?

Because when your life is uncertain, *certainty looks like a goal.* Even if it's fake.

Social media gives you front-row seats to everyone's "wins"—and none of their financial stress, credit card balances, or emotional costs.

And in your most vulnerable season, even one scroll can become a full-blown shame spiral.

Section 2: The Psychology of Social Comparison

You're not weak for comparing. You're human.

Social comparison is hardwired into us. It's how we:

- Gauge where we are
- Understand what's possible
- Feel motivated or connected

But in a world of curated feeds and constant updates, that wiring gets hijacked.

There are two types of comparison:

1. Upward Comparison

> *"They're ahead of me."*
>
> *This can inspire you—or discourage you.*

When you're healing from a breakup, it often leads to:

- Shame ("I should be further along")
- Panic ("I need to catch up")
- Spending ("Maybe if I buy this, I'll feel better")

2. Lateral Comparison

> *"They're just like me—but better off."*
>
> *This one can be brutal. Especially when it's your ex, a friend, or someone who* used to be in the same boat.

It tells you:

- "You're the problem."
- "You're the only one struggling."
- "Everyone else figured it out but you."

None of that is true. But if you're not aware of how comparison works, it can quietly shape your choices—and your bank account.

Section 3: How Social Media Fuels Financial Peer Pressure

Financial peer pressure used to be local. You'd see it at school, work, or church.

Now? It's global. Constant. Algorithmically delivered.

Every scroll says:

- "Buy this."
- "Upgrade now."
- "Success looks like this car, this outfit, this vacation, this kitchen."

But what social media rarely shows is:

- The credit card debt behind the luxury
- The stress behind the "dream job"
- The strained relationships under the surface

We're comparing our *real lives* to their *highlight reels.*

And when you're freshly divorced—emotionally raw, financially stretched—those reels can feel like judgment.

So let's build the tools to resist that pressure and protect your peace.

Section 4: Spot the Triggers—Before They Steer Your Wallet

Here's what emotional financial peer pressure might sound like in your head:

- "If she's traveling, I should treat myself too."
- "He already moved on and has a new house—I need to level up."
- "They'll think I'm struggling if I don't post something nice."
- "I deserve this after everything I've been through."

Let's break these down.

Trigger 1: The "Deserve" Trap

You've been through pain—and spending feels like a reward.

Reality check: You do deserve joy. But joy and debt aren't synonyms.

Trigger 2: The "Impress" Impulse

You want your ex, friends, or social media followers to see that you're thriving.

Reality check: Real thriving is internal. No one gets the full picture—except your bank account.

Trigger 3: The "Catch Up" Urge

You feel behind. You want to close the gap—fast.

Reality check: Your timeline is *not* their timeline. You're not late. You're *building.*

Section 5: Protecting Your Financial Peace in a World That Glorifies the Flex

You don't have to delete all your accounts or go off-grid to reclaim your mindset. You just need a few strategies to stay grounded when the digital world tries to shake you.

1. Curate Your Feed With Intention

Unfollow or mute accounts that make you feel "less than"—even if they're people you know.

Follow accounts that:

- Promote financial literacy

- Share healing journeys
- Make you laugh
- Ground you in real-life progress, not perfection

Remember: Your feed should feel like a safe neighborhood—not a constant sales pitch or a comparison battlefield.

2. Create a "Comparison-Free" Zone

Set boundaries around your scroll time. Try:

- No social media during your budgeting time
- 24-hour detox when you're feeling financially triggered
- Use apps like Freedom or AppBlock to limit access when needed

And when you feel the comparison creep in, say out loud:

> *"Their timeline is not my truth. I'm building something real."*

3. Build a Real-World Support Circle

Social media often replaces real community—but nothing can substitute lived connection.

Make space in your life for:

- Friends who respect your budget
- People who celebrate *non-monetary* wins (healing, courage, consistency)
- Conversations that normalize the mess and growth of real financial rebuilding

If you're surrounded by people who make you feel like "less" for saying no to brunch, debt is around the corner.

Section 6: When the Pressure Leads to Spending—How to Course Correct

Let's say you've already fallen into the trap. You overspent on something flashy, unnecessary, or to impress someone.

You are not a failure. You are *human.*

Here's how to bounce back:

Step 1: Own It Without Shame

> *"I made a choice that didn't align with my goals. That doesn't mean I'm done—it means I'm learning."*

Shame creates cycles. Honesty creates momentum.

Step 2: Do a Quick Budget Recalibration

- What did you spend?
- Where can you adjust this month to rebalance?
- Can you return, sell, or cancel anything?

Even one reset decision builds confidence.

Step 3: Track the Emotional Trigger

Journal or voice-note:

- What was I feeling before I spent?
- What was I hoping this purchase would fix?
- What else could I do next time?

You don't just need a tighter budget—you need a safer outlet for those feelings.

Step 4: Replace the Habit With a Ritual

Every time you feel tempted to spend out of comparison, do something else instead:

- Revisit your financial vision board
- Text your accountability partner
- Watch a YouTube video about debt freedom or investing
- Go for a walk and say an affirmation

Turn impulse into intention.

Chapter 34: When Divorce Happens Later in Life – Gray Divorce Financial Considerations

Introduction: Facing a New Chapter

Divorcing later in life—often referred to as "gray divorce"—brings its own set of emotional and financial complexities. After decades of shared life, assets, and dreams, the prospect of starting over can feel overwhelming. But with thoughtful planning and informed decisions, it's possible to navigate this transition and build a secure, fulfilling future.

In this chapter, we'll explore the key financial considerations unique to gray divorce, offering clear explanations, practical action steps, and compassionate support to help you move forward.

Understanding the Landscape of Gray Divorce

The Rise of Gray Divorce

Gray divorce is becoming increasingly common. According to the Pew Research Center, the divorce rate for adults aged 50 and older has roughly doubled since the 1990s.

Several factors contribute to this trend:

- **Longer life expectancies**: With more years ahead, individuals seek fulfillment and happiness in their later years.
- **Changing societal norms**: Reduced stigma around divorce allows individuals to prioritize personal well-being.
- **Financial independence**: Especially among women, increased financial autonomy empowers decisions to leave unsatisfying marriages.

Key Financial Considerations in Gray Divorce

1. Division of Retirement Assets

Retirement savings often represent a significant portion of a couple's wealth. Dividing these assets requires careful attention:

- **Qualified Domestic Relations Order (QDRO)**: This legal order is necessary to divide certain retirement plans, such as 401(k)s and pensions, without incurring taxes or penalties.
- **Individual Retirement Accounts (IRAs)**: While IRAs don't require a QDRO, it's essential to handle transfers correctly to avoid tax consequences.

Action Step: Consult with a financial advisor and attorney to ensure proper division and transfer of retirement assets.

2. Social Security Benefits

If your marriage lasted at least 10 years, you may be eligible to claim Social Security benefits based on your ex-spouse's earnings record:

- **Spousal benefits**: You can receive up to 50% of your ex-spouse's benefit if it's higher than your own.
- **Survivor benefits**: If your ex-spouse is deceased, you may be eligible for survivor benefits, which can be up to 100% of their benefit.

Note: Remarrying may affect your eligibility for these benefits.

Action Step: Contact the Social Security Administration to understand your options and maximize your benefits.

3. Health Insurance and Long-Term Care

Post-divorce, securing health insurance becomes crucial:

- **Medicare**: If you're 65 or older, you're likely eligible for Medicare. However, it doesn't cover all healthcare costs.
- **Supplemental insurance**: Consider purchasing Medigap or other supplemental policies to cover additional expenses.
- **Long-term care insurance**: This can help cover costs of assisted living or nursing home care, which are not covered by Medicare.

Action Step: Evaluate your healthcare needs and explore insurance options to ensure comprehensive coverage.

4. Housing Decisions

Deciding whether to keep or sell the marital home involves both emotional and financial considerations:

- **Affordability**: Can you manage mortgage payments, property taxes, and maintenance on a single income?
- **Downsizing**: Selling the home and moving to a smaller, more manageable property can free up equity and reduce expenses.

Action Step: Assess your housing needs and financial capacity to make an informed decision about your living situation.

5. Estate Planning Updates

Post-divorce, it's essential to revise your estate plan:

- **Wills and trusts**: Update these documents to reflect your current wishes and beneficiaries.
- **Powers of attorney**: Designate trusted individuals to make financial and healthcare decisions on your behalf if needed.
- **Beneficiary designations**: Review and update beneficiaries on retirement accounts, life insurance policies, and other assets.

Action Step: Work with an estate planning attorney to ensure your documents align with your new circumstances.

Building a New Financial Foundation

Creating a Post-Divorce Budget

Adjusting to a single income requires careful budgeting:

- **Track expenses**: Monitor your spending to identify areas for adjustment.
- **Prioritize needs**: Focus on essential expenses and reduce discretionary spending.
- **Plan for the future**: Allocate funds for savings, emergencies, and retirement.

Action Step: Develop a realistic budget that supports your current lifestyle and future goals.

Rebuilding Credit and Financial Independence

Establishing or improving your credit is vital for financial stability:

- **Check your credit report**: Identify any errors or areas for improvement.
- **Pay bills on time**: Consistent, timely payments boost your credit score.
- **Limit new debt**: Avoid taking on unnecessary debt during this transition.

Action Step: Create a plan to manage debt and build a strong credit profile.

Emotional Well-Being and Support

Divorce later in life can be emotionally taxing. Seek support to navigate this period:

- **Therapy or counseling**: Professional guidance can help process emotions and develop coping strategies.
- **Support groups**: Connecting with others experiencing similar situations provides comfort and perspective.
- **Social connections**: Maintain relationships with friends and family to combat isolation.

Action Step: Prioritize your emotional health by seeking support and engaging in activities that bring joy and fulfillment.

Conclusion: Embracing a New Beginning

While gray divorce presents unique challenges, it also offers an opportunity for growth and renewal. By addressing financial considerations with care and seeking support, you can build a secure, independent future.

Remember, you're not alone on this journey. With each step, you're creating a life that reflects your values, goals, and aspirations.

Chapter 35: Supporting Adult Kids Without Draining Your Future

The Balancing Act: Love, Loyalty, and Limits

You love them. Unconditionally. Fiercely. Forever.

Even though they're technically grown—maybe with degrees, jobs, or kids of their own—they're still your children. And when they struggle, you feel it. When they call for help, your instinct is to show up. And if you've been through a divorce, there's often an added layer of guilt or urgency that says:

> *"I need to be there for them more now." "They've already been through so much." "I don't want them to feel the effects of my divorce."*

But here's what we need to name right out of the gate:

Supporting your adult kids should not come at the expense of your own financial stability.

This chapter isn't about stopping your support. It's about *reshaping* it. It's about finding that sweet spot where your heart and your budget can both breathe.

Because your kids need you. But they also need the example of someone who's creating a secure future for themselves. And that starts with boundaries, communication, and clarity.

Section 1: Why It Feels So Hard to Say No

It's not just about money. It's about history. It's about the moments you couldn't give them everything. It's about the shame you might carry from the divorce. It's about wanting to protect them from financial pain—because you know what that feels like.

But here's the truth:

Saying "no" to a financially dependent adult child isn't abandonment. It's an invitation for them to grow.

And saying "yes" to everything? That doesn't build safety—it builds resentment, fear, and financial instability for *everyone.*

So let's talk about how to support without sacrificing.

Section 2: Common Forms of Financial Support (and Their Hidden Costs)

1. Paying Their Rent

- **Pros**: Provides stability, helps in a short-term crisis
- **Cons**: Easily becomes ongoing; reduces their urgency to increase income

2. Covering Phone Bills, Car Insurance, or Streaming Services

- **Pros**: Relatively low cost, can be a way to stay connected
- **Cons**: Normalizes dependency, rarely revisited or renegotiated

3. Co-Signing Loans or Credit Cards

- **Pros**: Can help them qualify or build credit
- **Cons**: You're legally responsible; can tank your credit if they default

4. Direct Cash Transfers

- **Pros**: Immediate help
- **Cons**: No accountability; becomes expected

Section 3: The Cost to You (That You Might Be Ignoring)

Supporting adult kids without a plan can quietly erode your:

- Retirement savings
- Emergency fund
- Debt reduction progress
- Peace of mind

And when your finances suffer, your options shrink. That might mean:

- Delaying your retirement
- Taking on extra work later in life
- Selling your home
- Becoming financially dependent on them later

That's not selfish to name. It's *responsible.*

Section 4: Creating a Support Framework That Works for Everyone

Step 1: Assess Your Financial Reality

Ask yourself:

- What can I *actually* afford to give—monthly, annually?
- What's my current retirement picture?
- What goals or needs will be affected by this support?

Step 2: Decide What You're Willing to Offer

Options include:

- A fixed monthly amount
- Temporary support for a set timeframe
- Paying for specific services (therapy, tuition, groceries)

Whatever you choose: **Put it in writing.** Not as a contract—as clarity.

Step 3: Communicate With Compassion

Let them know:

> *"I love you, and I want to support you. But I also need to protect my financial future. Here's what I* can *do, and here's what I can't."*

Make it a *collaboration,* not a command.

Step 4: Empower Their Growth

Encourage them to:

- Set a budget
- Increase their income
- Get career or financial coaching
- Apply for aid, grants, or assistance programs

You're not cutting them off. You're *coaching them forward.*

Section 5: Tools and Boundaries That Protect You Both

Financial Tools

- **Prepaid cards**: Help limit spending
- **Family budgets**: Shared documents to track contributions
- **Cash flow apps**: Mint, YNAB, GoodBudget

Emotional Boundaries

- No guilt language
- No secrecy
- Scheduled check-ins about money (not emergencies)

Section 6: When the Conversation Is Hard (Or They React Poorly)

They might:

- Get defensive
- Accuse you of not caring
- Play on guilt

Here's your script:

> *"I understand this is hard. It's hard for me too. But part of loving you is preparing for my future, and showing you how to prepare for yours. I'm not stepping away. I'm standing beside you as you build."*

Section 7: What If They're Struggling With Mental Health, Addiction, or Instability?

Support doesn't mean enabling. In these situations, money often *doesn't* help.

Instead:

- Offer resources (therapy, housing programs, support groups)
- Provide rides, groceries, or safe spaces
- Set limits *and* stay connected

Protect your boundaries *and* your compassion.

Section 8: Preparing for the Future (Without Assuming They'll Support You)

Don't count on them to take care of you if your finances falter—especially if they've been financially dependent on you.

Instead:

- Keep saving for retirement
- Maintain your own emergency fund
- Invest in long-term care planning
- Talk to a financial advisor about realistic income and support expectations

You can help them without becoming their future financial plan.

Final Reflection: Love With Limits Is Still Love

It's not easy to say no to your kids. Especially when your heart says yes and your bank account says otherwise.

But boundaries *are* love. Planning *is* love. Modeling stability *is* love.

When you care for yourself financially, you show them what strength looks like. When you help with clarity and limits, you teach them how to rise.

You are not failing them by drawing the line. You are preparing them—and protecting you.

And that, friend? That is powerful parenting, no matter their age.

Chapter 36: Investing Basics – What You Need to Know to Begin

Welcome to the Other Side of Stability

If you're here, reading this chapter, it means you've made it through the storm—or at least you're learning how to dance in the rain.

Divorce has a way of unearthing all our insecurities about money. And investing? That might have felt like a luxury in your previous life, something your ex handled, or something you thought was just for people with more time, more money, or more confidence than you.

But here you are.

And here's the truth:

You don't need a finance degree, a six-figure income, or a Wall Street mentor to begin investing.

You just need a willingness to learn, a steady mindset, and a few clear steps. This chapter is your guide.

Let's walk through what investing is (and what it isn't), how it fits into your new financial life, and what to do—step by step—to get started with clarity and confidence.

Section 1: What Investing Actually Is

Investing is the act of putting your money into financial tools—like stocks, bonds, or real estate—with the goal of growing it over time.

It is *not* about gambling. It is *not* about quick wins. It is *not* something reserved for the wealthy.

Investing is simply planting seeds in the right soil, and allowing time and consistency to do the rest.

You may already be investing if you have a 401(k), pension, or IRA. But even if you're starting from scratch, there's no better time to learn than now.

Section 2: Why Investing Matters More Than Ever After Divorce

When you've gone from two incomes to one, or you're rebuilding from a financial settlement, every dollar matters. But so does every decision.

Investing gives you:

- A way to rebuild retirement
- A chance to grow wealth passively
- Protection from inflation
- Options when life throws another curveball

Without investing, you're likely just saving—and savings alone often can't keep pace with the cost of living.

Investing is how you put your money to work. It's how you stop trading only time for money. It's how you build your future on *purpose.*

Section 3: Know the Basic Investment Types

1. Stocks

- Buying a small piece (share) of a company
- Higher risk, higher potential return
- Best for long-term growth

2. Bonds

- Essentially a loan to a company or government
- Lower risk, lower return
- Offers stability and income through interest

3. Mutual Funds

- A mix of stocks, bonds, or other assets
- Managed by professionals
- Great for beginners due to diversification

4. ETFs (Exchange-Traded Funds)

- Like mutual funds, but traded like a stock
- Often have lower fees
- Easy to access and diversify

5. Index Funds

- A type of mutual fund or ETF that tracks a market index (like the S&P 500)
- Low cost, passive management
- Ideal for hands-off investing

Section 4: Understand Risk and Time Horizon

Investing always involves some level of risk. But risk doesn't mean recklessness.

Ask yourself:

- When will I need this money?
- How much risk can I emotionally and financially handle?
- What's my goal: growth, income, preservation?

The longer your time horizon, the more risk you can typically afford to take. Short-term needs = safer investments. Long-term goals = room for more growth-focused investing.

Section 5: Step-by-Step Guide to Getting Started

Step 1: Build a Solid Foundation

- Pay off high-interest debt
- Build a 3–6 month emergency fund
- Know your monthly cash flow

Step 2: Choose Your Account Type

- **401(k)**: Offered through work; check if there's a match
- **IRA**: Individual Retirement Account; tax benefits
- **Roth IRA**: Grows tax-free; best if you're in a lower tax bracket now
- **Brokerage Account**: No tax benefits, but more flexibility

Step 3: Select Your Investments

Start with low-cost index funds or ETFs. You don't need to pick stocks. Use model portfolios or robo-advisors if unsure.

Step 4: Automate Contributions

Set it and forget it. $50 a month can grow significantly over time.

Step 5: Review Annually

Adjust for life changes, risk tolerance, and goals. Don't check daily. Wealth grows in *decades,* not *days.*

Section 6: Emotional Traps to Avoid

1. Trying to "Time the Market"

You won't beat it. Even pros don't. Stay consistent. Stay long-term.

2. Panic Selling

Market drops are normal. Don't make fear-based decisions.

3. Getting Advice from Social Media Gurus

If they're not licensed and your plan isn't personalized, proceed with caution.

4. Investing Before You're Ready

Build your emergency fund first. Cover your basics. Then invest.

Section 7: Tools, Terms, and Support Systems

Tools:

- **Vanguard, Fidelity, Schwab**: Trusted low-cost investment firms
- **Acorns, Betterment, Ellevest**: Robo-advisors
- **Morningstar**: Research

Helpful Terms:

- **Asset allocation**: How you spread your money across investment types
- **Diversification**: Reducing risk by not putting all your eggs in one basket
- **Compound interest**: Growth on your growth—the magic of investing
- **Expense ratio**: What you pay to own a fund; lower is better

Support:

- Financial advisor (fee-only fiduciary)
- Online courses
- Books: "The Simple Path to Wealth," "I Will Teach You To Be Rich"

Final Thoughts: You Are More Ready Than You Think

You don't have to be perfect. You just have to be *willing.*

Willing to learn. Willing to begin. Willing to stay the course.

Every great investor started with their first dollar. Every secure future started with an uncertain today.

You have what it takes. Not just to recover, but to *rise.* Not just to save, but to *build.*

This isn't about becoming someone else. It's about becoming the version of you who believes:

> *"I can create wealth on my terms. And I will."*

Let's keep going.

Chapter 37: What Is the Market, the Economy, and Everything Else You See on TV?

Welcome to the Noise: Understanding the Financial Headlines

You've probably heard it all by now:

> *"The market is crashing!" "The Fed is hiking rates again." "GDP is down, inflation is up, and the labor market is tightening!"*

If you've ever watched the news and felt your blood pressure spike or your stomach drop—you're not alone.

Post-divorce, it's easy to feel like the world is already spinning too fast. Add in the financial headlines, and suddenly it seems like every decision you make is either going to sink or save your future.

But here's the truth:

Most of what you hear on TV isn't meant to help you. It's meant to *keep you watching.*

This chapter is your decoder ring. We'll break down what the market *really* is, what the economy *actually* means, and how to filter out the noise so you can make calm, clear decisions for *your* financial life.

Section 1: What Even Is "The Market"?

Let's start with the basics.

When people say "the market," they usually mean the **stock market**. But that's actually made up of **multiple markets.**

The Stock Market = Ownership

When you buy a stock, you buy a piece of a company. When lots of people do this, and prices go up or down, that's the stock market moving.

There are indexes that track overall performance:

- **The Dow Jones**: 30 big U.S. companies
- **The S&P 500**: 500 large U.S. companies
- **The Nasdaq**: Focuses on tech companies

So when you hear "the market is down," it usually means these indexes have dropped—*but it doesn't mean your personal investments are doomed.*

Other Markets You Hear About:

- **Bond market**: Where people buy and sell government or corporate IOUs
- **Real estate market**: Buying/selling homes
- **Commodities market**: Gold, oil, wheat, etc.
- **Crypto market**: Digital currencies like Bitcoin

Each market works differently and reacts to different things. Your job? Understand which ones actually impact you.

Section 2: The Economy vs. The Market

These are *not* the same.

The Economy = The Big Picture

It's the total of all the goods and services we produce, buy, sell, and trade. It includes:

- Jobs (employment/unemployment)
- Wages
- Consumer spending
- Inflation
- GDP (Gross Domestic Product)

The Market = Investor Emotion

The market is part math, part mood. It can go up when the economy is bad. It can drop when the economy is strong.

Why? Because investors are always reacting to *expectations,* not just data.

Don't confuse volatility with reality.

Section 3: Why the News Sounds So Scary

Because fear sells. Because tension keeps you tuned in. Because nobody clicks on a headline that says: "Markets Doing What Markets Do."

They want drama. But you want *stability.*

The key is to stop reacting and start interpreting. Here's how.

Section 4: How to Read Headlines Without Losing Your Cool

Headline: "The Fed Raised Interest Rates Again"

Translation: The Federal Reserve is trying to slow inflation by making borrowing more expensive. This might:

- Make credit cards or mortgages cost more
- Slow down spending
- Affect stock prices (temporarily)

What to do: Revisit your budget. Lock in fixed-rate loans if you're planning a big purchase. Don't panic sell investments.

Headline: "The Market Lost 500 Points Today"

Translation: The Dow dropped—but that's out of over 30,000 points. That's less than 2%.

What to do: Check your diversification. Turn off the TV.

Headline: "Recession Fears Loom as GDP Slows"

Translation: Economic growth is cooling. That's not the same as collapse.

What to do: Avoid big lifestyle changes. Stick to your long-term plan.

Section 5: What Actually Matters to You

Most of the financial news is not personal. But here's what *is*:

- Your job/income
- Your expenses
- Your emergency fund
- Your investment timeline
- Your goals

If those are stable, *you* are stable.

Section 6: Building Your "Financial Focus Filter"

Here's a tool to help you block out the noise.

Ask yourself:

1. Can I control this?
2. Does this affect my personal plan?
3. Do I need to take immediate action?
4. Am I reacting emotionally?

If the answer is no to the first three—you're allowed to let it go.

Section 7: How to Stay Calm in a Storm

1. Diversify

Don't put all your money in one stock, sector, or strategy.

2. Automate

Auto-invest every month. Stay the course no matter what the news says.

3. Zoom Out

Look at your investments yearly, not daily.

4. Talk to a Pro

A good financial advisor helps you stay grounded.

Final Reflection: The Market Will Move—But You Don't Have To

You don't have to chase every headline. You don't have to understand every economic indicator. You don't have to feel financial fear every time someone on TV sounds panicked.

You just have to stay rooted in *your plan.*

You've already survived enough turbulence. Let this part of your life be about peace, power, and perspective.

Because the market will rise and fall. The economy will stretch and shrink.

But you? You're building something stronger. Something steady. Something that no headline can shake.

Keep going.

Chapter 38: Starting Over at Any Age – Your Financial Reset Button Exists

Let's Begin Again, Together

Maybe you're 35. Maybe you're 55. Maybe you're turning 70 this year and you just watched the life you built for decades shift under your feet.

Wherever you are on the timeline, if divorce has left you financially unmoored, this chapter is here to remind you of one powerful truth:

You are allowed to start over. And it is not too late.

Not too late to build wealth. Not too late to set boundaries. Not too late to rewrite the rules of what financial security looks like for *you.*

Whether you walked away from a marriage with very little, or you're just realizing how much you relied on someone else to carry the financial load, your restart is valid.

And it can be powerful.

Let's break down exactly how.

Section 1: Resetting Your Mindset Before Resetting Your Money

You're not starting from zero. You're starting from *experience.*

You know more about what you want, what you value, and what you never want to tolerate again. That's a strategic advantage.

So before we talk about numbers, accounts, and plans, let's clean house mentally:

Common Thoughts to Challenge:

- "It's too late for me."
- "I'll never catch up."
- "I'm bad with money."
- "I wasted too many years."

All of these are just *thoughts.* Not truths. And none of them belong on your new financial path.

Replace them with:

- "I'm capable of learning new things."
- "I know what stability feels like, and I can create it again."
- "This is my chapter to build something new."

You have nothing to prove to anyone. You only have to protect and honor *yourself.*

Section 2: Build a Foundation With What You Have

Let's talk about your starting line.

First, inventory everything:

- Income sources (job, benefits, alimony, pensions, side gigs)
- Savings and checking balances
- Retirement accounts
- Property or assets
- Debt balances

This is your snapshot. Don't judge it. Just look at it.

From here, we build.

Action Steps:

- Open a new checking account in your name only (if not done already)
- Create a basic budget: Income - Expenses = What's Left
- Prioritize an emergency fund (goal: 3–6 months of expenses)
- Automate savings—even $20 a month matters

Section 3: Resetting at Different Life Stages

In Your 30s:

- Focus: Career growth, paying down debt, starting retirement savings
- Pros: Time is on your side. Compound interest is your best friend.
- Cons: Divorce may have derailed early momentum. Use this time to build new habits.

In Your 40s:

- Focus: Mid-career planning, increasing retirement contributions, stabilizing after divorce
- Pros: Likely higher income. Still time to save and invest well.
- Cons: May feel "behind." But catching up is 100% possible.

In Your 50s:

- Focus: Debt reduction, maxing out retirement, long-term care planning
- Pros: Peak earning years, potential for second wind
- Cons: Less time before retirement = need for clarity and strategy

In Your 60s and Beyond:

- Focus: Asset protection, downsizing, optimizing Social Security, drawing income smartly
- Pros: Wisdom and perspective
- Cons: May feel fixed in income or overwhelmed by starting over late. But many rebuild wealth well into their 70s and 80s.

Section 4: The Financial Reset Toolkit

Tools You Can Use:

- **Budgeting apps**: YNAB, EveryDollar, Mint
- **Retirement catch-up contributions** (if over 50)
- **High-yield savings accounts**
- **Side income platforms**: Upwork, TaskRabbit, local consulting
- **Financial planners**: Especially fee-only fiduciaries

Boundaries You Can Set:

- Say no to financially supporting adult kids if it threatens your plan
- Limit social spending that triggers emotional or comparison-driven overspending
- Decline co-signing for loans or credit cards

Every yes to your future might require a few strong no's in the present.

Section 5: What About Retirement Now?

Divorce can delay, reshape, or completely reimagine retirement.

Start by asking:

- What age would I *like* to retire?
- What income sources will I have (Social Security, retirement accounts, rental income)?
- What lifestyle do I want in retirement?
- What might I need to adjust (housing, location, expenses)?

It's not about retirement age. It's about retirement *readiness*.

You might:

- Work longer (but in a more flexible or passion-driven way)
- Downsize to free up cash
- Travel differently, but still joyfully

Your reset button includes this stage too.

Section 6: Examples of Real Resets

- **Angela, 42**: Went back to school after divorce, started a new career, built a six-figure business within 10 years.
- **Reggie, 57**: Sold the marital home, downsized, and began investing for the first time. Retired at 66 with more saved than he ever imagined.
- **Denise, 61**: Thought she was "too late," but started a Roth IRA, paid off credit cards, and travels 3x a year debt-free.

These aren't fairytales. They're possibilities.

And they started exactly where you are now.

Final Reflection: You're Not Behind. You're Building.

You are not behind. You are not broken. You are not done.

This is your fresh start.

Your reset button isn't some mystical idea. It's your next decision. Your next budget. Your next boundary. Your next brave step.

You are allowed to rebuild. You are allowed to rise. You are allowed to dream forward.

No matter your age, your past, or your current balance sheet.

This is your time.

Let's keep going.

Synopsis – Part 6: Tools, Resources, and The Road Ahead

P*art 6: Tools, Resources, and The Road Ahead* is your reader's final chapter shift—from rebuilding to thriving. This section is the bridge between everything they've learned and the empowered, intentional life they're now equipped to live. It's not about wrapping things up with a bow—it's about putting real tools in their hands and showing them where to walk next.

This section reminds readers that their divorce isn't the end of their financial life—it's the rebirth of their financial voice.

Here, they'll learn how to:

- Use practical tools to manage money with confidence
- Choose the right financial advisors, platforms, and apps
- Protect themselves with checklists for insurance, estate planning, and credit monitoring
- Find support and community through online resources, courses, and professional networks
- Keep momentum going with annual reviews, goal-setting rituals, and mindset resets

Whether they're 31 or 61, readers will walk away from this section knowing that:

- There's always another step forward
- They are not alone, and they are not behind
- Financial independence isn't about being perfect—it's about being present and prepared

The Road Ahead isn't a destination—it's a mindset. This section leaves them with hope, direction, and the steady reminder that no matter where they started, what they lost, or how messy the past has been, they can still write the next chapter—and it can be powerful.

Chapter 39: Choosing a Financial Advisor – Pros, Cons, and Must-Ask Questions

The Courage to Ask for Help

Let's be real: After a divorce, you might feel like you have to figure it all out alone. You've already gone through attorneys, courtrooms, mediation, paperwork—it's understandable if you're tired of asking for professional help.

But your financial life? It deserves clarity, confidence, and a calm strategy. And a good financial advisor can be one of the most powerful allies you have as you rebuild.

This chapter is here to show you how to choose wisely—so you get the help you need, not another headache. You don't need to be a financial expert to work with one. You just need to know what to ask.

Section 1: Do You Even Need a Financial Advisor?

Let's start by answering the big question: **Do I need a financial advisor?**

You might benefit from an advisor if:

- You're overwhelmed by financial decisions post-divorce
- You've received a settlement or inheritance
- You want a retirement plan but don't know where to begin
- You're trying to manage debt and invest at the same time
- You need help organizing assets, taxes, or estate plans

You might not need one (yet) if:

- Your financial situation is very simple
- You're just starting to budget or pay down debt
- You want to DIY with books, podcasts, and free resources

Action step: Write down your top 3 financial stress points. If you feel paralyzed about them, it might be time to bring in professional help.

Section 2: Types of Financial Advisors

Not all advisors are created equal. Let's break down the major types so you know what you're getting into.

1. Fee-Only Fiduciary Advisors

- Paid by *you* (flat fee, hourly, or as a % of assets)
- Legally required to act in your best interest
- No commissions for products sold

2. Commission-Based Advisors

- Paid through sales of insurance or investment products
- May have incentives to recommend certain products
- Not always required to put your best interest first

3. Hybrid Advisors

- Earn both fees and commissions
- May offer comprehensive planning *and* sell products

Pro Tip: If they aren't a fiduciary, ask *why not.* You deserve full transparency.

Section 3: Pros and Cons of Hiring an Advisor

Pros:

- Saves you time and stress
- Personalized strategy
- Can help with taxes, insurance, retirement, investments, and estate planning
- Accountability partner to keep you on track

Cons:

- Cost (can be hundreds or thousands a year)
- Risk of poor advice from the wrong person
- Some advisors push products over planning

Ask yourself: What would peace of mind be worth to me? That's the real value of a *good* advisor.

Section 4: The Must-Ask Questions

Here's your go-to interview checklist:

1. "Are you a fiduciary?"

This should always be a YES.

2. "How do you get paid?"

Fee-only, commission, or hybrid? You have a right to know.

3. "Do you specialize in clients like me?"

Look for someone who works with divorced individuals, midlife planning, or retirement transitions.

4. "What services do you provide?"

Not all advisors do taxes, insurance, or debt help.

5. "How often will we meet?"

You want a relationship, not a transaction.

6. "Can you walk me through your process?"

Listen for structure, clarity, and real planning steps.

7. "What's your investment philosophy?"

Beware of hype or promises of fast returns.

8. "Who are your other clients?"

Not for names, but for general demographics.

9. "Can I see a sample financial plan?"

You want to see what you're paying for.

10. "What happens if I decide to leave?"

No one should lock you in.

Section 5: Red Flags to Watch For

- Vague answers about fees
- Pressure to buy insurance or annuities right away
- Overpromising returns
- Dodging the fiduciary question
- Can't explain things in plain English
- Bad reviews or no credentials

You deserve clarity. If you feel confused, that's a sign to pause.

Section 6: Credentials That Actually Matter

There are a lot of letters out there. These ones carry real weight:

- **CFP®**: Certified Financial Planner
- **ChFC**: Chartered Financial Consultant
- **CPA**: Certified Public Accountant (for tax-heavy planning)
- CDFA™: Certified Divorce Financial Analyst
- RIA: Registered Investment Advisor (firm-level)

Ask for a free consultation. Most offer one.

Final Reflection: You Deserve Support

Asking for help doesn't mean you're weak. It means you're wise enough to build a team.

Choosing the *right* financial advisor isn't about trusting someone blindly. It's about knowing the questions to ask, reading between the lines, and finding a partner who meets you where you are.

Your future is worth protecting. Your goals are worth mapping out. And your peace of mind? That's worth everything.

You don't have to navigate this alone.

The right help is out there. And now, you know how to find it.

Chapter 40: Building Your Dream Team – CPA, Attorney, Planner, Therapist

You Were Never Meant to Do This Alone

Divorce has a way of isolating you. One day, you're part of a household. The next, you're trying to remember your passwords, your PINs, your goals, your dreams—and you're doing it all solo.

But here's the good news: **You don't have to rebuild your financial life by yourself.**

In fact, you shouldn't.

The strongest people don't go it alone. They gather a team. They find experts, guides, and support systems that help them heal, strategize, and rise.

This chapter is about assembling *your* Dream Team. Not the expensive, intimidating, corporate one you might picture. But the *right-sized,* down-to-earth, practical team of professionals who can walk with you through this next chapter.

Let's break it down person by person.

Section 1: The CPA (Certified Public Accountant)

What They Do:

- Tax planning and filing
- Help with post-divorce income changes
- Manage alimony/tax reporting
- Business accounting if you're self-employed
- Guidance on estimated taxes, retirement withdrawals, and deductions

Why You Might Need One:

- Divorce can change your tax filing status
- You may now be self-employed or managing new income streams
- You want help avoiding surprise tax bills

Pros:

- Can save you money and reduce audit risk
- Keeps your financial records clean
- Often works with other professionals on your team

Cons:

- May charge by the hour or per return
- Not all CPAs are proactive planners

Action Steps:

- Look for CPAs with experience in divorce, small business, or retirement planning
- Ask: "Do you offer year-round planning or just filing?"

Section 2: The Attorney

What They Do:

- Draft or revise your estate plan (will, trust, power of attorney)
- Assist with legal matters post-divorce (custody, support modifications)
- Create business structures if you're starting a venture

Why You Might Need One:

- Your old estate plan names your ex as the decision-maker
- You want to protect your kids, assets, or future inheritance

Pros:

- Prevents future legal conflicts
- Ensures your documents reflect your new life

Cons:

- Can be costly
- Legal language can feel intimidating without good communication

Action Steps:

- Choose someone who explains things in plain language
- Ask: "Do you specialize in estate planning or family law?"

Section 3: The Financial Planner

What They Do:

- Help you set goals, invest wisely, and plan for the future
- Create budgets, retirement plans, and insurance strategies
- Coordinate with CPAs and attorneys

Why You Might Need One:

- You want someone to look at your full picture: income, expenses, goals, and dreams
- You're not sure how to invest, save, or plan alone

Pros:

- Offers clarity, direction, and emotional support through money choices
- Helps you build wealth on your terms

Cons:

- Varies in cost and credentials (see Chapter 42 for how to choose)

Action Steps:

- Look for a fee-only fiduciary planner
- Ask: "How do you support clients post-divorce?"

Section 4: The Therapist or Divorce Coach

What They Do:

- Help you process emotions around money, relationships, identity
- Provide strategies to manage stress, boundaries, and change
- Some specialize in financial therapy

Why You Might Need One:

- Divorce is emotional, and money is emotional
- You need to rebuild confidence, trust, and vision

Pros:

- Safe space to explore what divorce triggered in you financially
- Can help you understand old money patterns and build healthier ones

Cons:

- May not offer specific financial advice
- Finding the right fit can take time

Action Steps:

- Ask if they have experience with divorce or financial trauma
- Try 1-2 sessions before committing to long-term work

Section 5: How to Afford Your Team (Even on a Tight Budget)

Prioritize:

- Start with the support that meets your most urgent need (taxes, emotions, planning)

Ask About:

- Sliding scale rates
- Payment plans
- Pro bono or nonprofit services

Combine Resources:

- Use your planner's network to find an attorney
- Ask your CPA if they work with divorce professionals
- Join support groups that offer referrals

Your team doesn't need to be built all at once. Build brick by brick.

Section 6: Warning Signs to Avoid

- Anyone who won't answer pricing questions clearly
- Professionals who talk over you, not with you
- One-size-fits-all advice
- People who don't respect your story or boundaries

Your Dream Team should make you feel heard, respected, and supported.

Final Reflection: Build Your Life, With Your People

You don't have to know everything. You just have to know who to call.

Your Dream Team isn't about being dependent—it's about being *supported.* It's about learning to stand even stronger because you let the right people walk beside you.

Each person you bring into your corner is part of your comeback story. Each meeting, each question, each moment of clarity adds strength to your new foundation.

You're not doing this alone. You never were meant to.

Chapter 41: Financial Literacy Resources for Divorcees – Books, Podcasts, Websites

You Don't Have to Know Everything—Just Where to Look

When you're picking up the financial pieces after divorce, it can feel like you're staring down a thousand questions with no roadmap.

Where do I even start? Who can I trust? What does this term mean?

Here's the truth: **You don't have to do it all yourself. You just need to know where to learn.**

This chapter is a curated guide of tools, communities, and trusted voices to walk with you long after you close this book. Whether you like to read, listen, watch, or connect, there are resources that speak *your* language.

Let's build your financial bookshelf, earbuds playlist, and digital support team.

Section 1: Books That Can Change the Game

These books are clear, relatable, and powerful—no financial jargon required.

1. The Simple Path to Wealth by JL Collins

- Focus: Investing basics and long-term thinking
- Why it matters: Teaches you how to grow wealth without stress

2. You Are a Badass at Making Money by Jen Sincero

- Focus: Money mindset and confidence
- Why it matters: Great for overcoming fear or shame after divorce

3. I Will Teach You To Be Rich by Ramit Sethi

- Focus: Practical financial systems for real life
- Why it matters: Step-by-step plan for banking, saving, investing, and more

4. Your Money or Your Life by Vicki Robin & Joe Dominguez

- Focus: Aligning spending with your values
- Why it matters: Helps redefine what "rich" means on your terms

5. Breaking Money Silence by Kathleen Burns Kingsbury

- Focus: Financial conversations and emotional literacy
- Why it matters: Especially powerful for women navigating money shifts post-divorce

Bonus Picks:

- *Get Good with Money* by Tiffany Aliche
- *Money: A Love Story* by Kate Northrup
- *Smart Women Finish Rich* by David Bach
- *The Financial Wisdom of Ebenezer Scrooge* (for visual learners and story-

based readers)

Section 2: Podcasts That Talk Like a Friend

Plug in while you drive, cook, or walk. These hosts break it down so it actually makes sense.

1. HerMoney with Jean Chatzky

- Focus: Women and personal finance
- Why it matters: Encouraging, smart, and practical conversations

2. So Money with Farnoosh Torabi

- Focus: Money + life integration
- Why it matters: Diverse stories, actionable tips, real talk

3. Smart Passive Income with Pat Flynn

- Focus: Side income and online business
- Why it matters: Great if you're rebuilding career or income streams

4. The Money Guy Show

- Focus: Financial planning for every life stage
- Why it matters: Practical guidance, especially post-divorce

5. Afford Anything with Paula Pant

- Focus: Mindful spending, financial independence
- Why it matters: Encourages autonomy and value-aligned choices

Section 3: Websites and Communities That Walk With You

1. *Bogleheads.org*

- Community and wiki based on JL Collins-style investing
- Simple, low-cost, long-term strategies

2. *SmartHerMoney.com*

- Financial empowerment for women, especially after life transitions

3. *SavvyLadies.org*

- Free financial education and pro bono planning for women

4. *NAPFA.org*

- Find a fee-only fiduciary financial planner near you

5. *XYPlanningNetwork.com*

- Great for Gen X/Y clients, many virtual advisors available

6. *DivorceandMoney.com*

- Focused specifically on finances through the divorce process

7. *HelloDivorce.com*

- Legal + emotional support with financial guidance

Section 4: Tools, Templates, and Trackers

You don't need to build it from scratch.

Budgeting:

- **YNAB (You Need A Budget)**
- **EveryDollar**
- **GoodBudget**

Net Worth Tracking:

- **Personal Capital (now Empower)**
- **Tiller (spreadsheets for money nerds)**

Credit Monitoring:

- **Credit Karma** (free reports + insights)
- **Experian** (track and freeze credit, monitor for fraud)

Debt Management:

- **Undebt.it** (custom payoff plans)
- **Debt Free Charts** (visual progress tools)

Section 5: When You Want a Live Voice or Local Support

Try:

- Your local library (many host free workshops)
- Women's resource centers
- Divorce support groups
- Financial literacy nonprofits (like Operation HOPE or United Way)

Don't underestimate the value of *in-person encouragement.*

Section 6: How to Vet a New Resource

There's a lot of noise online. Use these filters:

- Is this person/product trying to *sell* me something immediately?
- Do they disclose fees or affiliations?
- Are they licensed or certified in any way?
- Does their content align with my goals—or just pressure me to spend?

Trust your gut. Your financial education should feel empowering, not overwhelming.

Final Reflection: You're Building a Lifelong Library

You don't need to consume everything. You just need to stay curious.

Pick one book. One podcast. One tool. One step forward.

Financial literacy isn't a one-time lesson. It's a lifestyle. It's how you take your power back—not all at once, but *consistently.*

With the right resources, you can:

- Learn in your own voice
- Make decisions with clarity
- Teach your kids, your friends, your community

You're not just recovering from divorce. You're rising as someone who knows their worth, their goals, and their options.

Let these resources walk with you. You don't need to rush. Just begin.

Your life. Your money. Your terms.

Chapter 42: Case Studies – Real Stories, Real Recoveries

Proof That You're Not Alone

This chapter isn't theory. It isn't statistics or strategy.

This chapter is real.

Real people. Real pain. Real turning points. And most importantly? **Real recovery.**

What you're about to read are stories of people who stood exactly where you're standing now: unsure, overwhelmed, financially anxious, and emotionally spent. Some were left with nothing. Some started with debt. Some had kids to raise, homes to leave, or lives to rebuild from the floor up.

But every single one of them did it.

Not because it was easy. But because they decided to begin.

These case studies are anonymous, but every story comes from someone who gave us permission to share so that *you* would feel a little less alone.

Let's begin.

Case Study 1: Angela – Starting Over at 42 With Two Kids and No Plan

Angela was married for 18 years. Her husband managed all the finances. When the divorce was final, she was left with primary custody of two kids, no savings, and a part-time admin job.

The Low:

Angela felt humiliated asking her parents for help. She didn't know where to begin—until her daughter asked, "Mom, are we going to be okay?"

That was her turning point.

The Rebuild:

- Angela got a free budgeting app (EveryDollar) and started tracking expenses.
- She found a local nonprofit that helped her create a resume and apply for jobs.
- Within 4 months, she landed a full-time role with benefits.
- She worked with a fee-only planner on a sliding scale to build a basic plan.
- She saved her first $1,000 in six months, cried, and then set a new goal.

Today:

Angela has an emergency fund, contributes to a 401(k), and speaks at local women's groups about financial confidence.

Case Study 2: Reggie – Debt, Divorce, and Downsizing at 57

Reggie had a six-figure job, but after divorce, he was left with a large alimony obligation, credit card debt, and a house he could no longer afford alone.

The Low:

He felt ashamed. As a man who "should have known better," he avoided asking for help.

The Rebuild:

- Reggie sold the house and moved into a smaller condo, using equity to pay off debt.
- He hired a financial therapist to work through money guilt.
- He maxed out catch-up contributions to his retirement plan.
- He built a realistic plan to retire at 67 instead of 62.

Today:

Reggie has a part-time consulting side hustle, enjoys cooking, and feels proud of the legacy he's now building for his grandkids.

Case Study 3: Priya – Immigrant, Single Mom, and Financial Phoenix

Priya moved to the U.S. at 29, married, had three children, and later divorced at 45. She had no credit history, no retirement savings, and worked part-time cleaning houses.

The Low:

Her ex left the country. She received no support. She had to rebuild alone, in a second language.

The Rebuild:

- Priya took a free financial literacy course at a community center.
- She opened a secured credit card and paid it off monthly.
- She started saving $10 per week and created a side business cooking for local families.
- She got a microloan to expand her catering services.

Today:

Priya owns a thriving local business and recently purchased her first home—with her name on the deed.

Case Study 4: Monica – Late-Life Divorce at 68

Monica had been married for 42 years. Her divorce came after retirement. She hadn't worked in over two decades, and their retirement funds were tied up in joint investments.

The Low:

She didn't know if she'd outlive her money or lose her home.

The Rebuild:

- She worked with a Certified Divorce Financial Analyst to understand her rights.
- She revised her estate plan and applied for Social Security under her

ex-spouse's record.
- She sold her large home and moved into a co-op community with friends.
- She took a financial workshop for retirees and set up a trust for her grandchildren.

Today:

Monica travels three times a year, volunteers at a community center, and mentors women through divorce recovery.

Final Reflection: Real People. Real Power.

These aren't perfect stories. They're *true* stories.

They include grief, debt, rebuilding, healing, and ultimately—a new kind of freedom.

Whatever your past has looked like, your future can look different.

Not because you hustle harder. Not because you win the lottery. But because you take small, steady steps with your own timeline, your own heart, and your own truth.

You have the right to rebuild. You have the power to begin.

Let these stories be your mirror, your map, and your motivation.

Chapter 43: The Annual Financial Calendar – What to Review and When

Rhythm = Relief

When you're recovering from divorce, finances can feel like a never-ending list of fires to put out. The unexpected bills, the paperwork, the changes in income, the re-learning of every account, every form, every deadline.

But once you've gotten through the triage? You deserve structure. You deserve rhythm.

Welcome to your **Annual Financial Calendar**—a month-by-month guide designed to give your financial life a calm cadence.

Think of this like meal-prepping for your money. A system that doesn't just react to emergencies, but proactively creates peace.

You don't have to do it all at once. Just know what matters when, and check in regularly.

This chapter will walk you through every season of the year with clear action steps, empowering insight, and a rhythm that will carry you confidently forward.

January: Set the Tone

Focus:

- Annual goals
- Budget refresh
- Tax prep begins

To-Do:

- Review your budget and create new savings goals
- Gather W-2s, 1099s, and other tax forms
- Review retirement account contributions and max them if possible
- Confirm automatic payments for all bills are active and accurate
- Update your net worth statement (assets – debts = net worth)

Empowering Insight:

New year, new mindset. You get to write this year's financial story with intention.

February: Check the Foundation

Focus:

- Insurance review
- Credit health

To-Do:

- Review all insurance policies (auto, home, health, life, disability)
- Make sure beneficiaries are updated post-divorce
- Pull your credit report (free at annualcreditreport.com)
- Dispute any errors
- Check your credit score with a trusted tool

Empowering Insight:

Foundations protect what you build. Give them attention.

March: Tax Time Strategy

Focus:

- Taxes
- Side hustle planning

To-Do:

- Organize all documents for your tax professional (or software)
- File early if you can
- If self-employed, prep for Q1 estimated taxes
- Evaluate if you'll owe or receive a refund
- If you get a refund, allocate it to goals: debt, savings, or emergency fund

Empowering Insight:

Your refund isn't free money. It's your money. Make it work.

April: Spring Clean Your Accounts

Focus:

- Subscription audit
- Investment check-in

To-Do:

- Cancel unused streaming, gym, or app subscriptions
- Review your 401(k), IRA, and brokerage accounts
- Rebalance if needed based on performance and risk tolerance
- Schedule a call with your advisor (if you have one)

Empowering Insight:

Don't let small leaks sink big plans.

May: Insurance Deep Dive

Focus:

- Health and life insurance

To-Do:

- Check your life insurance policy's adequacy (term or whole)
- Review your health plan expenses (are you overspending?)
- Compare quotes if you're overpaying for coverage
- Explore HSA or FSA options if applicable

Empowering Insight:

Insurance is self-care. Future you deserves protection.

June: Mid-Year Money Review

Focus:

- Progress check
- Mid-year adjustments

To-Do:

- Compare your actual income and expenses to your budget
- Adjust savings goals based on changes
- Celebrate any wins—even small ones
- Update your financial vision board or list

Empowering Insight:

A mid-year reset helps you finish strong. Course corrections are a sign of growth.

July: Legal and Estate Check-In

Focus:

- Will, trust, and POA
- Divorce decree compliance

To-Do:

- Review your estate plan
- Make sure your will reflects your post-divorce priorities
- Update Power of Attorney and medical directives
- Verify your ex is removed from all legal and financial designations

Empowering Insight:

This isn't morbid. It's empowering. It's love in legal form.

August: Back to School, Back to Basics

Focus:

- Family planning
- Education savings

To-Do:

- Review or open a 529 plan or education savings account for your kids
- Talk to your children (age appropriately) about money
- Revisit your childcare, tuition, or school budget

Empowering Insight:

Legacy starts with literacy. What you model, they inherit.

September: Recession-Proof Planning

Focus:

- Emergency funds
- Recession prep

To-Do:

- Reevaluate your emergency fund amount (3–6 months minimum)
- Practice a bare-bones budget—just in case
- Reduce unnecessary expenses for one month as a reset

Empowering Insight:

You can't predict the storm, but you can shore up your shelter.

October: Open Enrollment and Benefits

Focus:

- Employer plans
- Medicare or marketplace renewal

To-Do:

- Review employer health plans, FSA/HSA, disability, and life insurance
- Make selections for the next calendar year
- Review Medicare enrollment (if over 65 or eligible due to disability)
- Apply for ACA marketplace coverage if self-employed

Empowering Insight:

Benefits are money. Know them, use them, maximize them.

November: Gratitude + Giving Plan

Focus:

- Charitable giving
- Family conversations

To-Do:

- Plan and document any year-end giving (tax-deductible donations)
- Talk with your children, heirs, or beneficiaries about financial values
- Review your budget before holiday spending begins

Empowering Insight:

Giving with intention is powerful. Even $10 with clarity makes a difference.

December: Year-End Wrap-Up

Focus:

- Reflection and renewal
- Goal setting

To-Do:

- Review total income, debt progress, and net worth
- Celebrate what worked
- Journal lessons learned (financial and personal)
- Set your three biggest goals for the new year

Empowering Insight:

You are not the same person you were a year ago. And that's a good thing.

Final Reflection: This Is Your Rhythm Now

This calendar isn't rigid. It's a rhythm.

It's a tool for peace of mind. A map. A maintenance guide. A monthly moment to look at your money and say:

"I see you. I respect you. I'm paying attention."

That's what financial empowerment looks like in practice. It's not flashy. It's not instant. It's steady, quiet, powerful.

Month by month, decision by decision—you're not just surviving.

You're owning it.

Let's keep going.

Chapter 44: Questions to Ask Your Professionals

Ask Better. Live Better.

There is so much power in a good question.

When you're rebuilding your financial life after a divorce, you might find yourself talking to more professionals than ever before: lawyers, CPAs, financial advisors, therapists, estate planners, mortgage lenders. And every one of them speaks their own language.

If you don't know what to ask, it can be intimidating. You might nod politely in meetings, leave confused, and feel like you missed something important.

But that doesn't have to be your story.

This chapter is your toolkit for *how to ask smart, clear, confident questions* that get you the answers you deserve. Because professionals aren't just service providers. They are teammates. And you deserve to be the captain of your team.

Let's break it down, one expert at a time.

Section 1: Questions to Ask a Financial Advisor

Core Questions:

1. Are you a fiduciary? Will you always act in my best interest?
2. How do you get paid?
3. Do you work with clients who are divorced or in transition?
4. What is your investment philosophy?
5. How will we track my progress?
6. How often will we meet?
7. What services are included, and what might cost extra?
8. Will you help me understand this in plain language?
9. Can I see a sample financial plan?
10. What happens if I want to leave?

Empowering Insight:

A good advisor wants you informed. Not just invested.

Section 2: Questions to Ask a CPA or Tax Professional

Core Questions:

1. Are you a licensed CPA?
2. Do you have experience working with recently divorced individuals?
3. How do you bill—hourly, per form, or flat fee?
4. Can you help me plan for taxes, or just file them?
5. Will you help me understand how my divorce impacts my filing status?
6. Can you explain how alimony or child support affects my taxes?
7. Should I be paying quarterly taxes?
8. Are there deductions or credits I may be missing?
9. Will you help me with retirement account decisions?
10. How do you prefer to communicate—email, calls, portal?

Empowering Insight:

Taxes are not a mystery. They're just math with context.

Section 3: Questions to Ask a Divorce Attorney or Family Law Attorney

Core Questions:

1. How do you bill? Can I get an estimate of total costs?
2. What is your experience with cases like mine?
3. What are my rights, and what are my risks?
4. Can you explain the divorce decree to me in plain English?
5. What do I need to keep an eye on post-divorce?
6. Will you work with my financial planner or CPA if needed?
7. Are there legal deadlines I should calendar?
8. Can I get copies of everything for my records?
9. What if my ex doesn't comply with the agreement?
10. How do I update my name or beneficiaries legally?

Empowering Insight:

The legal system is complex. But your questions don't have to be.

Section 4: Questions to Ask a Therapist or Financial Therapist

Core Questions:

1. Do you have experience working with divorce, grief, or financial trauma?
2. Are you licensed, and what is your therapeutic approach?
3. How often should we meet?

4. Will we focus more on processing emotions, or building strategies?
5. Are you comfortable discussing money-related anxiety or guilt?
6. Do you offer sliding scale pricing or insurance billing?
7. What are common emotional patterns you see in divorced clients?
8. Can we explore old money beliefs that may be holding me back?
9. How will I know if I'm making progress?
10. What does a successful outcome look like in your eyes?

Empowering Insight:

Your emotions around money deserve just as much attention as your numbers.

Section 5: Questions to Ask an Estate Planning Attorney

Core Questions:

1. Do I need a will, a trust, or both?
2. Who should be my Power of Attorney and medical proxy now?
3. What happens if I don't update my beneficiary forms?
4. How often should I review my documents?
5. What happens to my kids or pets if something happens to me?
6. Can I set up protections for my children's inheritance?
7. What's the difference between a living will and an advance directive?
8. How do I make sure my ex doesn't end up with control again?
9. What are the legal requirements in my state?
10. What will this cost, and what's included?

Empowering Insight:

Estate planning is about love, not fear.

Section 6: Questions to Ask a Mortgage Broker or Real Estate Pro

Core Questions:

1. Can I qualify for a mortgage on my income alone?
2. Should I rent or buy in my current financial situation?
3. What's the real cost of owning this home?
4. Can you help me understand my credit score and how to improve it?
5. Are there loan programs for recently divorced individuals?
6. How much house can I afford without being house-poor?
7. What are your fees or commissions?
8. Will my spousal support or child support count as income?
9. What happens if I want to refinance later?
10. How fast do I need to act if I see a home I like?

Empowering Insight:

A home is shelter—but it's also a strategy. Don't buy based on emotion alone.

Final Reflection: Questions Are Currency

Asking the right questions is a sign of power. Not weakness.

The world of post-divorce finances is full of terms, tools, and transitions. But the greatest advantage you can bring into every room, every office, every Zoom meeting?

Curiosity. Clarity. Courage.

You don't have to know all the answers. You just have to ask the right questions.

And now? You know exactly what those are.

Let your voice be heard. Let your team rise with you. And let your future begin with one confident, clear, and bold question at a time.

Chapter 45: Conclusion – Your Divorce Isn't the End, It's the Rewriting of Your Wealth Story

Let's stop right here and take a breath together.

You made it. Through the thick of it. Through the grief, the paperwork, the confusion, the anger, the stress, the sleepless nights, the splitting of furniture, and the splitting of dreams. You got through 47 chapters of hard truths, financial pivots, emotional resets, spreadsheets, boundaries, and budget rebuilds.

But this last chapter? This one's not just about the money. This is about *you*. About what happens *after* the storm clears. When the silence settles. When the calendar doesn't revolve around court dates or mediation. When your name is once again yours alone.

This is the part where we talk about what's next.

Because no matter how tired you are, or how uncertain the path ahead might feel, I want to make one thing clear:

Your divorce is not the end of your story. It's the beginning of your financial rebirth.

Let's Acknowledge the Grief, First

You can't heal what you haven't faced.

Before we charge ahead with account setups and asset strategies, we need to name what divorce *really* does—not just on paper, but in your heart.

Divorce can shatter trust—not just in your ex, but in yourself.

It can make you doubt every financial decision you've ever made. It can make you ashamed for not knowing what was going on in the joint accounts. It can make you angry for giving up your career to stay home. Or exhausted by how many sacrifices you made while someone else got to walk away with the better credit score or more stable paycheck.

And underneath all of that?

Grief.

Grief for the life you planned. Grief for the stability you thought you had. Grief for the version of you that didn't get to grow inside that relationship.

So before we rebuild anything, let's take a quiet second to say: *I see you.* I see the version of you who did the best they could with what they knew. I see the love you gave, the compromises you made, the risks you took, the hope you held.

And I see the you that's standing here now—ready to write a new chapter. One that belongs only to you.

The Power of a New Financial Identity

Let's talk about something that doesn't show up in credit reports or estate plans: financial identity.

When you were married, your financial identity was likely tied up in someone else's. Joint goals. Joint decisions. Joint consequences. Maybe you managed the money. Maybe they did. Maybe it was somewhere in between.

But now?

Now you get to decide who you want to be, financially.

Are you the woman who finally opens her own investment account at 48? The man who pays off a credit card for the first time in years and swears never to carry a balance again? The parent who teaches their kids about money with wisdom born from heartbreak? The partner who's ready to set financial boundaries with clarity and confidence in their next relationship?

You get to choose.

Divorce doesn't just dissolve a marriage. It dissolves a *financial identity* that wasn't working for you anymore.

This is your chance to build one that fits who you really are.

What We've Learned (And What You're Taking With You)

Let's take a look at the financial tools you've picked up along the way. These aren't just lessons—they're building blocks.

You Now Understand:

- How to budget based on your *real* income and *real* expenses
- How to create an emergency fund that gives you breathing room
- The difference between wants and needs—and when to honor both
- What credit really means, how to rebuild it, and how to protect it
- How to understand your retirement options and rebuild your nest egg
- How to separate finances with care and protect your financial identity
- How to say "no" with love—and boundaries
- How to shop smarter, invest wisely, and insure intentionally
- How to plan for your future, without needing a partner to do it

And most of all?

You've learned that your financial power isn't about perfection.

It's about *participation*.

Rewriting Your Wealth Story—On Your Terms

Now let's talk about your wealth story.

Wealth is not just about money. It's not just about how much you have in your retirement accounts or whether you own or rent.

Wealth is about how you *feel* about your money.

It's about agency. Confidence. The ability to choose what matters to you and let go of what doesn't. It's about legacy, security, dignity, and peace of mind.

Divorce may have torn a few pages out of your financial playbook. But that doesn't mean the story is over.

You are still the author. And the next chapter? It's yours to write.

Here's what that might look like.

Step One: Reaffirm Your Financial Vision

Now that the dust has settled, it's time to come back to yourself.

Ask Yourself:

- What kind of lifestyle do I want in five years?
- What kind of financial experiences do I want to create?
- How do I want to feel when I log into my bank account?
- What do I want to model for my kids, friends, or community?

You don't have to answer all of these today. But write them down. Sit with them. Let your intuition talk.

You've spent years responding to someone else's priorities. Now, it's your turn.

Step Two: Create a Post-Divorce Financial Bucket List

You've handled the basics. Now let's start dreaming again.

What are some financial milestones or experiences that are just for you?

Here are some ideas to get you started:

- Open a Roth IRA and max it out for the first time
- Take a solo vacation you fully paid for
- Buy your own home with your name alone on the deed
- Get completely debt-free
- Start a side hustle that brings in extra income

- Fund your child's college with confidence
- Build a "freedom fund" so you can walk away from anything that doesn't serve you

Action Step:

Write a list of 10 financial milestones you'd like to hit in the next 5–10 years. Big or small. Concrete or emotional. This is your new bucket list.

Step Three: Practice Future-Focused Financial Thinking

It's easy to get stuck looking backward after a divorce.

- "I wasted so much time."
- "We should have invested earlier."
- "If only I hadn't left my job."
- "I'll never recover from this."

Pause.

Let's try something different.

Start asking yourself: *What does future me need?*

Future You wants peace. Wants options. Wants financial decisions that honor their mental and emotional health—not just their spreadsheet.

So when you're deciding whether to say yes to a big purchase, a new job, a move, or a relationship, ask:

- Will this support the person I'm becoming?
- Will this decision bring me closer to stability or take me further from it?
- Am I acting from fear, or from freedom?

That's wealth thinking. That's rewriting your story.

Step Four: Pass the Wisdom On

One of the most beautiful things about financial healing is this: you get to become a light for others.

You may not feel like a teacher right now. But just by reading this book, just by taking these steps, you've already become someone who *knows more than you used to.*

You can share that.

With your kids. Your friends. Your coworkers. Your next partner.

You can speak from scars, not wounds. You can normalize having honest money conversations. You can encourage someone to check their credit, set a budget, protect themselves legally, or ask for help.

Action Step:

Think of one person in your life who could benefit from what you've learned. Write them a note. Send them a chapter. Offer to be a sounding board.

You're not just rewriting your wealth story. You're helping others rewrite theirs, too.

Step Five: Remember—You Are the Asset

Your home isn't your greatest asset.

Your car isn't.

Your retirement account isn't.

You are.

Your skills. Your resilience. Your ability to pivot and rebuild. Your willingness to learn and grow. Your values. Your presence. Your faith. Your support system. Your ability to love and trust again.

Money can be rebuilt. Homes can be resold. Careers can be restarted. Relationships can be reimagined.

But your *sense of self-worth*? That's priceless.

So as we close this chapter—and this book—let's end on this note:

You are not broken.

You are not behind.
You are not starting over with nothing.
You are starting over with *everything you've learned.*

Step Six: Healing Through Financial Empowerment

Financial recovery after divorce is not just about cleaning up the mess. It's about reclaiming your *power.*

When you make your first solo budget, that's empowerment.

When you check your credit score and face it head-on, that's empowerment.

When you say, "I can't afford that right now" without guilt or shame? That's real power.

Healing and Wealth Go Hand-in-Hand

So often we talk about healing in emotional or relational terms—but rarely do we talk about financial healing. And yet the two are so deeply connected.

If your marriage had financial control, secrecy, manipulation, or misalignment, you may carry invisible wounds around money.

- Maybe you learned to be small with your spending so your partner wouldn't get angry.
- Maybe you spent impulsively as a form of rebellion or escape.
- Maybe you gave up your financial dreams to keep the peace.

Whatever your past relationship with money looked like, you're allowed to create a new one.

Action Step:

Write a forgiveness letter—to yourself. Forgive yourself for the debt, the overspending, the missed red flags, the fear. Then write a second letter: a declaration of the relationship you now want to have with money. Keep both somewhere safe.

Step Seven: Build Long-Term Habits That Stick

You've made progress. You've learned the tools. Now it's time to sustain the momentum.

Here's how to make sure this work sticks with you long after the last page.

1. Set a Monthly "Money Day"

Choose one day each month to do your financial check-in. Put it on the calendar like an appointment.

On Money Day, you can:

- Review your budget
- Look at your spending and saving
- Check your progress on goals
- Celebrate wins, no matter how small
- Adjust where needed

Consistency builds trust—with yourself.

2. Automate What You Can

Set up:

- Auto-pay for fixed bills
- Automatic transfers to savings or investment accounts
- Auto-investment into a retirement or brokerage account

Automation is the antidote to chaos. It keeps your progress going, even when life gets hard.

3. Track Your Net Worth Every Quarter

Net worth = what you *own* minus what you *owe*.

It's a simple number, but watching it grow—even slowly—can be deeply motivating.

Use a notebook, a spreadsheet, or apps like Mint, Empower, or YNAB. Just keep it consistent.

4. Keep Learning

Pick one financial book, blog, podcast, or course to dive into each quarter. Stay connected to your growth.

You don't need to know everything. You just need to stay curious.

Step Eight: Watch for the Emotional Saboteurs

Even with a solid plan, there will be moments when old patterns creep in. That's okay. It doesn't mean you're failing. It means you're human.

But let's name the emotional saboteurs so you can spot them when they show up.

1. Guilt Spending

You might feel the urge to over-give to your kids, family, or friends to "make up" for the divorce.

The Truth: Your presence and peace are more valuable than any gift.

2. Revenge Spending

"I gave up everything for them, now I deserve this!"

And you do deserve joy—but joy built on resentment rarely brings peace.

The Truth: Empowered spending is rooted in love, not anger.

3. Comparison Traps

You'll scroll Instagram and see your ex on vacation or in a new home. You'll see friends who didn't go through what you did—and it'll sting.

The Truth: You're building *real* wealth—emotional, spiritual, and financial—not highlight reels.

4. Scarcity Spiral

You may panic about the future. You may hoard money or avoid looking at your accounts.

The Truth: Looking gives you power. Clarity is not the enemy—it's your ally.

Action Step:

Make a list of your top 3 money triggers. Next to each one, write a new affirmation or boundary to anchor yourself when it shows up.

Step Nine: Define What "Rich" Means to You

The world will try to define wealth for you: how big your house is, what kind of car you drive, where your kids go to school, what labels are in your closet.

But that's not *your* definition—unless you choose it.

Let's write a new one.

Here are some prompts to get you started:

- I feel rich when I…
- I know I'm secure when…
- My version of success includes…
- I want to build a life where…

Maybe rich, to you, is being able to take your grandkids to the zoo without checking your bank balance.

Maybe it's waking up without debt.

Maybe it's sleeping in on a Tuesday in a home you paid for.

Maybe it's knowing no one else gets to tell you how to spend, save, or earn ever again.

Action Step:

Finish this sentence in your journal: "My richest life looks like..." and write for 5 minutes without stopping. Let your truth rise to the top.

Step Ten: Consider Your Legacy—Because You Still Have One

Divorce can feel like it disrupts everything—even the story you wanted to leave behind.

But your legacy didn't end with your marriage. In fact, it may have *just begun.*

Financial Legacy Isn't Just Inheritance

Legacy includes:

- Teaching your children about budgeting, credit, and resilience
- Leaving behind clarity with a well-drafted will or trust
- Donating to causes that mattered to you
- Documenting your story so others can learn from it
- Modeling what healing and rebuilding can look like

You don't need millions to leave a legacy. You just need *intention.*

Action Step:

Write a one-page "Letter of Financial Wisdom" to the next generation—or even to your future self. What would you want them to know, remember, or avoid?

Step Eleven: If You Love Again, Do It Differently

Many divorcees eventually find love again—and some of them get remarried.

If that's in your future, wonderful. But go in with eyes wide open and boundaries strong.

Things to Talk About Before Sharing Finances Again:

- Credit scores and debt
- Spending styles
- Financial goals
- Past mistakes and money triggers
- Whether you'll keep accounts separate, joint, or hybrid
- Prenups and estate planning (especially for blended families)

You've Been Through Too Much to Skip the Money Talk

Love is powerful. But it's not a financial plan.

Let love in—but bring your financial boundaries with you.

Action Step:

Make a "Relationship & Money" checklist of questions you'd want to ask a future partner *before* joining finances. That's called *financial self-respect.*

Final Reflections: You Are Not Alone

You're not the only one figuring out how to navigate life after divorce.

Millions of others—many who would never speak of it publicly—are quietly rebuilding too.

You're not behind.

You're not broken.

You're not financially ruined.

You are *becoming.*

You are stepping into your role as the lead character in your wealth story. Not the sidekick. Not the second income. Not the silent partner. The author. The voice. The visionary.

And even though you didn't plan this chapter, you have the power to shape how the rest of the story goes.

About the Author

Patrick Brown, MBA, is a financial advisor, educator, and advocate for those rebuilding their lives after life-changing transitions—especially divorce. With over two decades of experience in wealth management, retirement planning, insurance, and financial literacy, Patrick brings more than just credentials to his work—he brings heart.

His passion for financial education began on a deeply personal level. After witnessing the impact of financial confusion and emotional overwhelm in his own family and community, Patrick made it his mission to become a trustworthy, relatable voice in the world of personal finance.

Patrick is the founder of multiple financial education platforms, including *Financial Literacy For Divorcees,* which was built to serve the unique and often overlooked needs of those navigating the emotional and financial fallout of divorce. Through this book and others in his growing financial literacy series, he empowers people to take back control of their money and rewrite their wealth story with clarity and confidence.

A former Division I athlete and CFL football player turned trusted financial professional, Patrick combines discipline with compassion. He knows what it's like to start over—and what it takes to keep going.

Today, Patrick continues to guide individuals and families through every season of life, offering steady mentorship, practical tools, and the kind of financial wisdom that doesn't just teach—it heals.

When he's not writing or advising, Patrick enjoys family time with his wife and daughters, community service, public speaking, and inspiring others to take the next right step—financially and personally.

Should You Work with a Financial Advisor After Divorce?

Understanding the Pros, Cons, and What Makes Sense for You

Divorce can leave you carrying more than just emotional weight—it often means managing your finances solo for the first time in a long time. Between budgeting, retirement planning, insurance updates, and tax filings, it can be hard to know what to prioritize or how to put the pieces back together.

For many newly single individuals, hiring a financial advisor can offer structure, clarity, and much-needed peace of mind. But it's not the right choice for everyone—and that's okay. The key is understanding what an advisor does, what it costs, and whether it fits *your* needs and goals right now.

Pros of Working with a Financial Advisor

1. Guidance Across All the Moving Parts

A qualified financial advisor can help with everything from rebuilding your retirement strategy to understanding your tax implications post-divorce. They can help you restructure investment accounts, review insurance needs, update beneficiaries, and even manage the emotional side of money—all in one place.

2. Saves Time and Reduces Stress

When you're recovering from divorce, decision fatigue is real. A financial advisor helps take complex tasks off your plate and simplifies the process so you can focus on your healing, your family, and your future.

3. Helps You Avoid Emotional Mistakes

Money decisions made in panic or grief can have long-term consequences. A trusted advisor acts as a steady voice of reason—helping you stay focused, avoid impulsive choices, and stick to a long-term plan that reflects your new goals.

4. Keeps You Accountable

Life after divorce can be messy. A financial advisor helps keep you on track with everything from updating legal documents to staying on top of savings goals. You don't have to do it all alone—they'll follow up when life gets busy.

5. Customized, Personal Planning

Divorce is not one-size-fits-all, and neither is good financial advice. A great advisor will tailor your plan based on your income, debts, custody agreements, career goals, and dreams for your next chapter.

Cons of Working with a Financial Advisor

1. There's a Cost

Advisors typically charge either a percentage of the assets they manage (usually 0.5%–1%), a flat annual fee, or hourly rates. If you're still recovering financially or have limited assets, that fee may feel steep—especially if you're not receiving hands-on support.

2. Quality Varies (A Lot)

Not all advisors are fiduciaries (which means they're required to act in your best interest). Some may earn commissions from the products they recommend. It's important to ask the right questions and understand exactly how your advisor is paid.

3. You Still Need to Be Involved

Even with a great advisor, you'll need to stay engaged. Your input, your goals, and your values matter. Think of it like hiring a personal trainer—you'll still have to show up and do the work.

4. Risk of Cookie-Cutter Advice

Some advisors rely on templated strategies or model portfolios that don't reflect your specific needs. If they don't take time to understand what's changed in your life since the divorce, the advice may fall flat.

5. DIY May Be Enough for Some

If you're financially savvy, enjoy learning about personal finance, and your needs are fairly straightforward, you might do just fine managing your finances yourself. With modern apps, online tools, and budget templates, DIY is more accessible than ever.

So... Should You Hire a Financial Advisor?

Here are a few questions to help you decide:

- Do you feel overwhelmed or unsure about what to focus on first?
- Are you juggling investment accounts, insurance decisions, legal documents, and new living expenses?
- Do you have kids, a business, or other responsibilities that add complexity?
- Do you simply want someone to walk this path with you—so you don't have to figure it all out alone?

If you answered yes to any of these, a financial advisor might be a worthwhile investment in your peace of mind.

Final Thought: You Deserve a Plan—and a Partner

You've already walked through one of life's most difficult transitions. Your financial future deserves to be steady, intentional, and supportive of who you're becoming—not who you used to be.

A good financial advisor won't just give you spreadsheets or investment tips—they'll give you perspective, confidence, and guidance that reflects *your* values. And if you're not ready to work with an advisor just yet? That's okay too. Just keep moving forward. You're doing better than you think.

Disclaimer

Financial Literacy For Divorcees was written to educate, empower, and encourage individuals who are navigating the emotional and financial complexities of life after divorce. The insights in this book are based on the author's personal experience, professional training, and over two decades of work in financial services, personal development, and educational outreach.

That said, it is important to clarify what this book *is*—and what it *is not*.

For Educational Purposes Only

This book is intended for general educational and informational purposes. It is designed to provide those going through or recovering from divorce with foundational financial knowledge, tools for responsible decision-making, and awareness of common challenges and opportunities in post-divorce financial life.

While this book includes strategies, case examples, and financial principles, it is *not* personalized advice. Your financial journey is unique. Your income, assets, debts, custody agreements, tax status, health needs, and long-term goals will vary significantly from those of other readers.

Before making any major financial, legal, or business decisions, consult directly with qualified professionals licensed to provide tailored advice.

No Legal Advice

Although this book touches on legal topics that are often involved in divorce—such as property division, spousal support, child support, or estate planning—it does not constitute legal advice. It is not a substitute for working with a licensed attorney.

If you are:

- Navigating a divorce settlement or mediation
- Creating or modifying a custody or support agreement
- Drafting or updating a will, trust, or power of attorney
- Starting or ending a business after divorce
- Managing legal liability related to shared debts or property

…you should seek legal counsel from an attorney familiar with family law, estate planning, or business law in your state.

Laws and obligations vary widely based on location and circumstances. Only a licensed attorney can ensure your legal rights and responsibilities are protected.

No Financial or Investment Advice

This book is not written by a Certified Financial Planner™, Registered Investment Advisor, or licensed broker-dealer. While it offers ideas, frameworks, and general financial strategies, it does not provide personalized investment recommendations or financial planning advice.

If you are considering:

- Investing in specific financial products
- Developing a retirement withdrawal plan
- Rebalancing your investment portfolio
- Buying or selling real estate post-divorce
- Making changes to insurance or annuity contracts

...you should speak with a licensed financial professional—especially one experienced in working with divorcees or high-transition life stages.

No results or outcomes are guaranteed. Investment decisions carry risk, and all readers are responsible for their own financial choices.

No Accounting or Tax Advice

Although taxes often play a significant role in the financial aftermath of divorce, this book is not authored by a CPA, enrolled agent, or licensed tax preparer.

If you:

- Need help understanding the tax impact of alimony, child support, or property division
- Are filing taxes for the first time post-divorce
- Receive income from multiple sources or states
- Own a business, side hustle, or investment property
- Are exploring tax-advantaged retirement strategies

...you should consult a licensed tax professional. Only a qualified accountant or preparer can determine the best filing strategies, ensure your compliance with IRS rules, and minimize your audit risk.

Any mention of tax concepts in this book is for awareness purposes only.

No Guarantees or Promises

Reading this book does not guarantee financial success, stability, or wealth. Every individual's circumstances, choices, behaviors, and outcomes are different.

Any case studies, examples, or numbers presented in this book are meant to illustrate concepts—not to predict actual results or imply any specific financial outcome.

Progress after divorce is deeply personal. What worked for one person may not work for another. What matters most is that you stay committed to growth, clarity, and empowerment over time.

Limitation of Liability

By reading this book, you agree that the author, Patrick Brown, MBA, and all affiliated platforms—including *FinancialLiteracyForDivorcees.com* and related brands—are not responsible for any decisions or outcomes you experience as a result of using the content in this publication.

The author and affiliated entities disclaim liability for any financial losses, legal disputes, tax consequences, or other personal or business impacts related to the material presented.

You are solely responsible for your financial decisions.

Build a Support Team

The author believes strongly that every individual rebuilding their life after divorce deserves access to a trustworthy team of professionals—including a financial advisor, attorney, therapist, tax professional, and insurance consultant.

This book is designed to complement—not replace—that team.

If you haven't yet built your team, consider this your invitation to begin. Healing from divorce isn't just emotional—it's financial, too. With the right guidance, you can recover, rebuild, and reclaim your peace of mind.

You've already made it through one of the hardest seasons of your life. Now it's time to create a financial future that honors your strength—and supports your next chapter.

Your Post-Divorce Financial Calendar

A Month-by-Month Guide to Staying Organized, Empowered, and Proactive

When you're managing money on your own—possibly for the first time in years—it can feel like you're constantly trying to catch up. This calendar is designed to help you stay ahead. Each month brings key tasks, deadlines, and planning moments to keep your finances healthy, your documents in order, and your stress levels down.

Let's take it one step at a time. This isn't about perfection. It's about consistency, confidence, and clarity as you move forward.

JANUARY

January 1

- New contribution limits go into effect for retirement accounts: 401(k), 403(b), 457, IRA, and Roth IRA.
- HSA and FSA limits reset—review and adjust if needed.
- Begin the year with a fresh budget and cash flow review.
- Update paycheck withholding (Form W-4) if your filing status, dependents, or income has changed.

January 15

- 4th Quarter Estimated Taxes Due for prior year income (October 1 – December 31). Use IRS Form 1040-ES.

Late January

- W-2s, 1099-NEC, 1099-MISC, 1099-INT, 1099-DIV, and 1099-B begin arriving from employers, clients, banks, and brokerages.

FEBRUARY

February 1

- Deadline for employers and payers to issue W-2s and 1099s.

Mid to Late February

- K-1s from partnerships or S-corps may arrive (some come later).
- Begin gathering your tax documents or upload them to your CPA.

MARCH

March 15

- Partnership and S-Corp tax returns due (Form 1065 or 1120-S).
- File an extension using IRS Form 7004 if needed.

March 31

- Deadline to receive electronic Forms 1095-A/B/C (proof of health coverage).

APRIL

April 1

- If you turned 73 last year and delayed your first Required Minimum Distribution (RMD), today is your deadline to take it.

April 15 *(or next business day if it falls on a weekend/holiday)*

- Personal Tax Filing Deadline (IRS Form 1040).
- 1st Quarter Estimated Taxes Due.
- Last day to make prior-year contributions to:
- Traditional IRA or Roth IRA
- SEP IRA (unless extension)
- HSA
- Coverdell ESA
- Deadline to file an extension (IRS Form 4868).
- FAFSA deadline in some states if applying for college financial aid for your child.

MAY

Early May

- Review your property tax assessment if applicable. Protest deadlines usually fall mid-month, depending on your state.

May 29 – National 529 Day

- Review or open a 529 College Savings Plan for your children or grandchildren.

JUNE

June 15

- 2nd Quarter Estimated Taxes Due.
- U.S. Citizens living abroad: tax filing deadline (automatic extension to October 15 available).

Mid-June

- Review retirement account performance. Adjust contributions if needed.
- Revisit charitable giving plans for the year.

JULY

July 1–15

- Mid-year financial check-in:
- Revisit your budget and savings goals.
- Check debt payoff progress.
- Rebalance investment portfolio if it's off target by more than 5–10%.
- Schedule a mid-year meeting with your financial advisor or CPA.

AUGUST

August 1–31

- Start preparing for fall open enrollment.
- Review your HSA and FSA balances.
- Revisit insurance coverage: life, disability, malpractice, umbrella.
- Begin planning for year-end charitable giving (DAFs, appreciated stock, QCDs if 70½+).

SEPTEMBER

September 15

- 3rd Quarter Estimated Taxes Due.
- Deadline for extended tax filings for Partnerships and S-Corporations.

Late September

- Consider backdoor Roth IRA conversion strategies.
- Begin reviewing investment losses for potential tax-loss harvesting before year-end.

OCTOBER

October 1

- Deadline to establish a SIMPLE IRA for current tax year.
- Medicare Open Enrollment Preview window opens.

October 15

- Deadline for filing extended individual tax returns (Form 1040 with extension).
- Deadline to fund prior-year SEP IRA (if you filed an extension).
- Deadline to recharacterize a prior-year Roth IRA contribution.

Late October

- Review employer open enrollment materials. Decide on health plans, HSA/FSA contributions, and other benefits.

NOVEMBER

November 1–30

- ACA Health Insurance Open Enrollment begins.
- Employer open enrollment typically happens now—review:
- Health plans (choose HSA-eligible if beneficial)
- Life & disability insurance

- 401(k) contribution levels
- FSA and HSA elections
- Legal or supplemental benefits

Black Friday Weekend

- Consider big purchases in light of year-end cash flow, tax deductions, or business expenses.

DECEMBER

December 1–15

- Final weeks to max out:
- 401(k), 403(b), and 457 contributions
- HSA contributions
- Backdoor Roth conversions
- Make final charitable donations for current tax year.

December 31 – Year-End Deadlines

- Take RMDs if age 73+.
- Make tax-deductible donations and fund Donor-Advised Funds (DAFs).
- Harvest capital losses to offset gains.
- Complete any backdoor Roth IRA conversions.
- Gift up to $18,000 per person (annual gift tax exclusion).
- Spend down remaining FSA balances (or check for rollover/grace period).
- Finalize any bonuses or profit-sharing distributions for business owners.

Bonus: Rolling & Event-Based Reminders

Every Paycheck:

- Verify 401(k)/403(b) deductions.
- Confirm correct health, dental, and HSA payroll deductions.

After Major Life Events:

Update accounts, beneficiaries, and financial plans after:

- Divorce or remarriage
- Birth/adoption of a child
- Job or contract changes
- Disability or health diagnosis
- Change in residence
- Receiving an inheritance or large windfall

Quarterly:

- Review your spending plan and budget.
- Make estimated tax payments if applicable.
- Rebalance your investment portfolio.
- Meet with your advisor if doing tax-loss harvesting or converting IRAs.

Final Tip: Automate What You Can

Set calendar reminders.

Automate retirement and savings contributions.

Use recurring bill pay.

Keep a running financial task list by month or quarter.

Life after divorce can be unpredictable. But your finances don't have to be. The more structure you build, the more peace you'll create.

You don't have to manage everything at once. You just need to keep showing up—month by month.

Made in the USA
Monee, IL
04 November 2026

67387591R00216